The New School Counselor

Strategies for Universal Academic Achievement

Rita Schellenberg

ROWMAN & LITTLEFIELD EDUCATION
Lanham • New York • Toronto • Plymouth, UK

Published in the United States of America
by Rowman & Littlefield Education
A Division of Rowman & Littlefield Publishers, Inc.
A wholly owned subsidiary of The Rowman & Littlefield Publishing Group, Inc.
4501 Forbes Boulevard, Suite 200, Lanham, Maryland 20706
www.rowmaneducation.com

Estover Road
Plymouth PL6 7PY
United Kingdom

British Library Cataloguing in Publication Information Available

Library of Congress Cataloging-in-Publication Data

Schellenberg, Rita Cantrell.
  The new school counselor : strategies for universal academic achievement / Rita
Schellenberg.
      p. cm.
  Includes bibliographical references and index.
  ISBN-13: 978-1-57886-834-6 (pbk. : alk. paper)
  ISBN-10: 1-57886-834-3 (pbk. : alk. paper)
  eISBN-13: 978-1-57886-912-1
  eISBN-10: 1-57886-912-9
  1. Educational counseling—United States. 2. Student counselors—United
States. I. Title.
  LB1027.5.S253 2008
  371.4'220973—dc22   2008020289

∞^{TM} The paper used in this publication meets the minimum requirements of
American National Standard for Information Sciences—Permanence of Paper for
Printed Library Materials, ANSI/NISO Z39.48-1992.

To my Father, for His favor

*To John, for so many years of
patience, love, and encouragement*

*To my parents, for your
unconditional love*

To my family and friends, for strengthening me

Contents

Preface

The need for leadership in school counseling has never been more evident. Persistent role ambiguity and a lack of shared accountability for academic achievement have resulted in limited alliances with school administrators and the continued exclusion of school counselors from educational reform initiatives.

Reform-minded counselor educators and school counseling practitioners are working diligently to transform the profession using a new vision and an academic- and systems-focused paradigm that aligns school counseling with the academic mission. The fundamental goal of the initiative is to reverse the direction of a young profession that is viewed as lacking in preparation, practice, and leadership, and ancillary to the academic goals of schools.

Although reform-minded leadership from within the school counseling profession is necessary, it is not sufficient to alter the landscape of school counseling—we simply cannot do it alone. Ultimately and undeniably, legitimization, institutionalization, and realignment of school counselors' roles and functions in public education are enormously, if not entirely, dependent upon division level school boards, superintendents, and school principals.

Administrators seek to use the specialized knowledge and skills of school personnel. Thus, school administrators realize that aligning school counseling programs with academic achievement agendas is valuable and central to school reform efforts and universal proficiency. However, the austerity of confusion and disagreement regarding the disjointed roles and functions of the school counselor have tainted efforts to attach this area of educational, developmental, and mental health expertise to the school system.

For the first time in history, elementary and secondary school counselors have clearly defined functions, preparation standards, and practice models, as well a professional paradigm congruent with that of school administrators. Although the professions differ, school counselors and school administrators are facing unprecedented challenges. Both must effectively manage change that results in higher levels of academic performance for all students in an educational system that is developing at exponential rates. School counselors and administrators are being called upon to demonstrate systemic and collaborative leadership and make efficient use of resources, manpower, and technology while personalizing the school environment. Finally, school counselors and administrators are required to achieve greater accountability with data-driven, standards-based, and research-supported curriculum and instruction.

Indeed, the soil is fertile for developing a united leadership between school counselors and school administrators. This striking partnership has the potential to position school counselors in the mainstream of school improvement and to positively influence the school counseling profession, educational systems, and, foremost, the future of our children.

Leadership and the effective use of human resources require a lucid understanding of school personnel roles and functions. Although the school counseling profession has made some progress in this area, the roles of school counselors have not been concretely established and there is no real distinction between school counselor roles and functions. Also interfering with reform progress is a paucity of practical alignment approaches and data reporting tools for implementing accountable and academic- and systems-focused school counseling programs.

This text assists school administrators, school counseling supervisors and practitioners, and counselor educators in developing a deeper understanding of the academic- and systems-focused paradigm and new vision for school counseling. Unlike others, this book is a *how-to-do-it* text that provides approaches and tools for implementing change and guiding the application of new vision theory in practice.

This text advocates for a paradigm switch from the traditional mental health– and individual-focused model to an academic- and systems-focused model that promotes the school counselor's dual roles of educator and mental health provider. The dual roles of the new school counselor are conceptualized and operationalized under the new paradigm and strategies for universal academic achievement are introduced.

The chapters that follow promote the transformation of school counseling around several themes to create comprehensive school counseling programs that promote universal achievement in a pluralistic society. Essential themes for developing a practical workable plan for change that delivers school counseling from a peripheral service to a vital educational program include the following: accountability; collaboration; leadership; universal academic achievement; instruction, curriculum, and assessment; advocacy; systemic change; research; rigorous standards; data and data reporting; standards; evaluation; systems integration; and technology. These themes are fundamental to best practices and significant in defining the future of a young and evolving profession in accordance with the American Association of School Administrators (AASA, 2007), American School Counselor Association *National Model* (ASCA, 2005), Council for Accreditation of Counseling and Related Educational Programs (CACREP, 2001), National Association of Elementary School Principals (NAESP, 2007), National Association of Secondary School Principals (NASSP, 2006), National Education Association (NEA, 2006), No Child Left Behind (NCLB, 2001), Transforming School Counseling Initiative (TSCI, Education Trust, 1997), and the U.S. Department of Education (1996, 2004).

This text provides a distinction between school counselor roles and functions that is in line with school missions, educational reform movements, and the new vision for school counseling. Conceptualization of the dual roles of the school counselor as both educational specialist and mental health specialist is presented for guiding contemporary preparation and authentic practice.

This text introduces *standards blending*—a systems-focused, integrative, and student-centered approach that directly and overtly aligns school counseling programs with academic achievement missions. The alignment occurs by methodically identifying and blending specific core academic standards with school counseling standards. As a primary and fixed appendage to a comprehensive developmental school counseling program, standards blending is the embodiment of academic- and systems-focused school counseling. Standards blending can be delivered as a systems support mechanism using schoolwide class-room guidance curriculum and as a responsive services strategy using small groups and individual counseling as recommended by the ASCA and AASA.

Mathematics and language arts were selected as the core academic content areas for standards blending because *reading, writing*, and *arithmetic* have always been basic to schooling and establishing a solid educational foundation. In addition, reinforcing language arts and mathematics standards assists schools in meeting the goal of reading and math proficiency by the 2013–2014 school year as set forth by NCLB (2001) and, thereby, the professional leadership of school counselors and administrators. The National Mathematics Standards (NCTM, 2000), Standards for the English Language Arts (NCTE, 1996), and the National School Counseling Standards (Campbell and Dahir, 1997) were selected because individual states use these standards to create more specific local standards, making them applicable to educators across the nation.

In addition to a nationally recognized standards foundation, impact data were collected to assess the meaningfulness of the standards blending. The evaluative study revealed significant knowledge development for minority and nonminority participants on both the school counseling and academic curriculum (Schellenberg, 2007).

As an integrative and student-centered approach to learning, standards blending encourages students to get involved, explore, discuss, discover, connect, and personalize the content. Standards blending promotes the application of differential instruction, assessing students' needs, and accommodating students' unique learning profiles, interests, and readiness. Standards blending also accommodates multiple categories of learning during instructional planning and delivery promoting Bloom's Taxonomy. The holistic and constructivist nature of the standards blending approach is indicative of a brain-based teaching strategy that is compatible with brain-based learning.

Standards blending is a practical and potentially powerful approach that provides students with a means by which to improve comprehension by connecting curricula and visualizing the interrelationships of learning and real life. Students are given the opportunity to socially interact with the curriculum, fellow students, and teachers in small learning communities where information is processed and problems are examined, deconstructed, and resolved. Such approaches have been linked to the development of background knowledge, intrinsic interest, and higher-order intelligence, as well as greater academic achievement and a heightened motivation toward learning (Marzano, 2004; Sink, 2005; Vansteenkiste, Lens, and Deci, 2006).

This text also introduces a groundbreaking, comprehensive electronic data reporting system that uses Microsoft Office forms to guide pre-service and currently practicing school counselors through the process of accountable programming from conception to evaluation. The system, provided on the enclosed CD, meets the essential component guidelines for action planning, closing the achievement gap, and results reporting recommended by the American School Counselor Association.

The *School Counseling Operational Plan for Effectiveness* (*SCOPE*) links directly to files that contain the national standards for mathematics, language arts, and school counseling as well as data sources for needs assessment and program evaluation. The *School Counseling Operational Report of Effectiveness* (*SCORE*) contains an Excel graph for colorful illustrations, and a worksheet with protected formulas for easy data analysis.

The information in this text is easy to follow and describes systemic, integrative, student-centered, and academic-focused programming. Chapters emphasize and illustrate needs- and data-driven practices, standards-based and research-supported curriculum, measurable outcomes, data reporting, and strategies for closing the achievement gap — hallmarks of new vision school counseling and school reform initiatives. Each chapter includes relevant research, literature, key players, and major developments and trends shaping contemporary school counseling.

Real world applications presented in this text bridge new vision theory and practice, providing counselor educators with experiential learning tools for optimal school counselor preparation. School administrators find this brief resource helpful in fulfilling their leadership function in integrating system components and providing educators with tools and approaches that support greater accountability and academic-focused student services. In the hands of school counselors, *The New School Counselor: Strategies for Universal Academic Achievement* is an essential, child-first guide to the metamorphosis of school counseling in the new millennium.

1

No School Counselor Left Behind

School counseling has been largely shaped by social justice movements and educational reform initiatives that flow like tides driven by congressional flavor. Still, the profession has been cautious, even reluctant, to comply with educational reform agendas that focus exclusively on academic achievement. The time is now, however, to throw caution to the wind, not only because of the rising of political and social tides, but because continuing to practice school counseling from the current paradigm is detrimental to a profession that is viewed as inadequately meeting the educational needs of students—the fundamental mission of schools.

No Child Left Behind (NCLB, 2001), the educational reform du jour, is considered by many to be the most significant and controversial educational reform legislation in our nation's history. The overarching goal of NCLB is to close the achievement gap between low-income and minority students and their more affluent peers on a national level. NCLB requires that educators engage in needs assessment strategies, and use scientifically based research and rigorous standards in curriculum development and delivery. Programming and assessment practices must be documented to reflect accountable practices in elementary and secondary educational programs for data-driven decision-making.

The concept of closing the achievement gap is not unfamiliar to school counselors, who have persistently strived to ensure the success of all students. The bigger issue for school counselors, however, is the indirect nature in which they go about accomplishing this task.

Studies reveal that school counselors have, for the most part, viewed their function as indirectly increasing the academic achievement of students by removing physical, personal, social, emotional, and behavioral obstacles to learning using primarily "individual-focused interventions on behalf of selected students" (Eschenauer and Hayes, 2005). Conversely, school administrators believe that the school counselor should function more systemically and "work with students to build skills that have a direct effect on school related work and functioning" (Shoffner and Williamson, 2000, p. 128).

Contradictory role expectations, coupled with a failure to directly align programs with academic achievement and provide data that demonstrate the positive impact of such programming, have hampered efforts to establish crucial leadership alliances with school administrators. Such deficiencies have interfered with school counselors' ability to secure a position on the educational team. Therefore, school counselors have been benched by legislators and school administrators in the challenge to educate America.

In short, school counseling programs are viewed as nice but not necessary, creating an immediate need for significant changes in counselor education and in the field. The gap between new vision theory and practice must be closed to reverse the dire trajectory of the school counseling profession. Altering the course of school counseling is paramount to providing students with the highest quality educational services and to ensure that no school counselor is left behind. Ralph Waldo Emerson may have said it best: "This time, like all other times, is a very good one, if we but know what to do with it."

FORCES SHAPING AN EVOLVING PROFESSION

Transforming School Counseling Initiative and ACA

The impetus behind the fundamental changes currently underway in school counselor education and practice was prompted by a report published in 1987 by the American Counseling Association (ACA), *School Counseling: A Profession at Risk*. The undeniable and disturbing realities regarding a profession viewed as withering and unnecessary prompted immediate, vigorous, and unremitting action on the part of concerned school counselor educators and practitioners.

The American School Counselor Association (ASCA) began creating monographs, position papers, role statements, revised program philosophies, and a series of recommendations to include school counselors as key players in educational reform. The ASCA adopted national standards (Campbell and Dahir, 1997) and a national model (ASCA, 2005), discussed later in this chapter. The Education Trust (1997) in collaboration with DeWitt Wallace–Readers Digest and the ASCA, the Association for Counselor Education and Supervision (ACES), and the ACA, introduced the Transforming School Counseling Initiative (TSCI).

The TSCI redefined the roles and functions of the school counselor within the context of a new vision for school counseling programs that more appropriately reflects the academic mission of schools. The TSCI introduced a new paradigm to replace the existing paradigm and immediately began emphasizing the importance of school counseling leadership, support for academic- and systems-focused programming, and the need to make adequate yearly progress.

The new paradigm shifts the focus of school counseling away from mental health and toward academic achievement, away from the individual student and toward the whole school. Those attached to the traditional mental health–focused paradigm argue that the new paradigm is too academic-focused, ignoring the mental health needs of students, while proponents of new vision school counseling argue that the new paradigm improves services to meet the mental health needs of students.

> Contrary to some interpretations, this new vision school counselor does not represent an abandonment of concern for the personal and social development of children and adolescents. Instead, it reflects the requirement that school counselors link interventions to the mission and purposes of schooling while holding themselves accountable for their contributions to student outcomes. (Paisley and Hayes, 2003, p. 200)

New vision school counseling requires a belief in the capacity of all students to obtain high levels of academic achievement and meaningful futures in a global economy and technologically advanced world. New vision school counselors engage in systemic leadership, advocacy, collaboration, counseling, coordination, assessment, and data analysis. Serving as social action agents, new vision school counselors identify and remove inequities and other barriers to academic achievement.

New vision school counselors align school counseling activities with the academic achievement mission of schools. The application of new vision school counseling requires knowledge and skills in developing and evaluating programs that are needs- and data-driven, standards-based, research-supported, and academic- and systemic-focused. Programming also includes strategies for closing achievement gaps. This new breed of school counselor is obligated by the professions of counseling and education, to not only demonstrate, but document accountable practices through the creation and dissemination of action plans and results reports. What school counselors should know and be able to do in order to implement the change needed for accountable, academic- and systems-focused service delivery must be taught and reinforced in both education and practice.

School counselor training programs prior to standards-based educational reform movements generally applied a clinical, mental health pedagogy and an individualistic focus with little or no emphasis on standards, systems, technology, the use of data, academic achievement, program evaluation, evidence-based practices, and data reporting. Therefore, many currently practicing school counselors lack the preparation and understanding of the roles and functions of the contemporary, academic-focused school counselor and, thereby, the tools and approaches for new vision programming. What's more, since practice informs academic theory, paradoxically, deficits in practice are creating deficits in school counselor education resulting in the absence of new vision applied approaches and models for the optimal preparation of future school counselors.

While the TSCI was actually established with the express purpose of restructuring school counselor education at the graduate level, the TSCI recognized the need to close this preparation gap between school counselors trained under the traditional model and those trained under the new vision model. For that reason, the TSCI partnered with Metropolitan Life Insurance Company (MetLife) to fund the development of the National School Counselor Training Initiative (NSCTI) and the National Center for Transforming School Counseling (NCTSC).

The NSCTI and NCTSC developed and disseminated four modules that instruct practicing school counselors in the components of the TSCI new vision. The modules challenge school counselor belief systems and describe how school counselors can contribute to the high academic achievement of and obtain educational equity for all students through both systemic and individual leadership, advocacy, and collaboration.

The MetLife initiative also addresses systemic inequities, social justice, diversity, accountable practices, and technological competence.

Center for School Counseling Outcome Research

Addressing the need for school counselor leadership in establishing accountable practices, the *Center for School Counseling Outcome Research* (CSCOR, 2000) was established during a TSCI summer conference. The Center is part of the University of Massachusetts Department of Student Development and Pupil Personnel Services of the School of Education. CSCOR focuses on providing resources to assist school counselors in grounding practices in research and standards, conducting program evaluation, and administering valid outcome measures. The center publishes quarterly research briefs for school counseling practitioners to increase knowledge regarding ways in which school counselors can implement academic- and systems-focused practices and support strategies for closing the achievement gap.

CSCOR supports the TSCI's new vision for school counseling and promotes the principles and school improvement initiatives of the American Association of School Administrators (AASA), ASCA, Council for Accreditation of Counseling and Related Educational Programs (CACREP), National Association of Elementary School Principals (NAESP), National Association of Secondary School Principals (NASSP), No Child Left Behind (NCLB), and the U.S. Department of Education.

CSCOR advocates for new vision school counseling and the implementation of accountable practices by (a) assisting efforts to ensure that all students achieve academically, (b) emphasizing the importance of systemic interventions, and (c) focusing on the importance of using research to guide practice, monitor effectiveness, and evaluate student learning outcomes.

School Counseling Leadership Teams

In 2001, in an effort to advance the movement to transform school counseling, a reform-minded group of counselor educators, school counseling supervisors, and organizational leaders established the School Counseling Leadership Team (SCLT) in northern Virginia. The primary goal of the SCLT is to reinforce the efforts of the TSCI and ASCA by rallying support for reform-minded leadership essential to the development of accountable academic- and systems-focused school counseling.

Using communication, collaboration, and advocacy at all levels, the SCLT has already effected much change in Virginia. Efforts of the SCLT have resulted in revised standards for school counseling programs in Virginia public schools, which had not been updated since 1984, reinstatement of the position of school counseling specialist for the Virginia Department of Education, which had been vacant for over eight years, and the passage of legislation that requires every public elementary school in Virginia to have a school counselor.

Additionally, the SCLT conducts workshops and educational summits to school counselors, directors of school counseling, and administrators to increase knowledge pertaining to accountability strategies and the new vision academic-focused roles and functions of school counselors. The value of the SCLT in propelling efforts to achieve school counseling reform is clearly evident.

Kaffenberger et al. (2006) offer guidelines for establishing a powerful SCLT. Recommendations include a collective membership that is representative of all primary stakeholders; strong leadership; needs-based, goal-focused activities; and a means for internal evaluation.

Association for Counselor Education and Supervision and CACREP

The Association for Counselor Education and Supervision (ACES) is a division of the American Counseling Association. The purpose of ACES is to provide leadership and continuous improvement in the education, credentialing, and supervision of counselors in diverse work settings. Committed to the advancement of counselor education and supervision, ACES began the accreditation of counseling programs, which laid the foundation for its successor, the Council for Accreditation of Counseling and Related Educational Programs (CACREP).

In 1978, CACREP was formed to standardize training and function as the primary accrediting body for counselor education programs, under the prevailing school counseling pedagogy of the time, which was mental health–focused. The 2001 CACREP Standards, currently under revision for implementation in 2009, reflect the new vision, academic- and systems-focused paradigm. The CACREP Standards serve as unified, minimal competencies for the optimal preparation of school counselors.

While CACREP has now provided consistency in school counselor education with rigorous and unified standards, historically, school counselor education programs have been inconsistent in the preparation of school counselors. Inconsistencies in preparation have prolonged role confusion, perpetuated variations in professional practices, and hindered the ability to firmly establish a unified professional identity. Recovering from past practices has been slow, with some of the most current research indicating that the majority of principals still struggle to understand the roles and functions of the school counselor requisite to judiciously integrating school counseling into the educational system (Chata and Loesch, 2007).

CACREP requires demonstrated knowledge in eight core areas of counselor education (i.e., professional identity, social and cultural diversity, human growth and development, career development, helping relationships, group work, assessment, and research and program evaluation) in addition to the requirements specific to counseling in the schools. The CACREP Standards specific to school counseling reflect the educational reform climate, emphasizing education and training in developing evidence-based practices for diverse and special-needs students, academic outcomes, the identification and removal of personal and systemic barriers to academic achievement, and demonstrated knowledge in the use of needs assessments, data, program evaluation, and technology in counseling practices.

As of 2007, 50 to 60 percent of eligible counselor education programs have been accredited by CACREP. Many school counselors have completed programs that follow the CACREP Standards, but it is not indicated on their degree since CACREP accreditation acknowledgment is afforded only to those students, who graduate after or within one year prior to when accreditation is conferred rather than the date that the program was in compliance with the CACREP Standards. This is particularly evident in inaugural programs whereby students follow the CACREP Standards. Programs can validate that students completed CACREP requirements, but because the accreditation process took longer than one year from the students' date of graduation, these students cannot claim graduation from a CACREP accredited program.

Therefore, it is recommended that school administrators and school counseling supervisors assessing the qualifications of school counselors consider CACREP equivalency and the level of a school counselor's knowledge pertaining to CACREP. School counselors who understand the importance of CACREP generally list the accreditation and/or note that the program was CACREP track on their application/resume.

Counselors who hold the voluntary National Certified Counselor (NCC) credential from the National Board for Certified Counselors (NBCC) have demonstrated mastery of the CACREP Standards as well as the NBCC standards. Therefore, school counselors, who hold the NCC credential have established equivalency to graduation from a CACREP accredited program as well as mastery of the high standards set by the profession.

National Board for Certified Counselors

Gladding (2001) defines certification as the process by which an agency, government, or association officially grants recognition to an individual for having met certain professional qualifications that have been developed by the profession. NBCC is the national professional certification board that monitors the certification system for counselors and maintains a national register of certified counselors. In addition to national credentialing, NBCC examinations are used by more than forty-eight states to credential professional counselors on a state level. NBCC was created by the American Counseling Association and both organizations work closely to advance the profession of counseling and maintain high standards of excellence.

The NBCC administers specialty counseling credentials such as the National Certified School Counselor (NCSC) credential first awarded in 1991. The NCC is a prerequisite or corequisite for the NCSC. School counselors who hold the NCSC have demonstrated competence in areas specific to contemporary school counseling and demonstrate a high level of professional commitment that goes beyond required state licensing.

The NBCC requires a master's degree and uses the CACREP Standards, the ASCA program standards, formal practices statements, and national studies to create NCSC requirements and assessment. The NCSC is a product of a collaborative effort between key professional counseling organizations and supported by CACREP and ACES.

The NBCC and the National Board of Professional Teaching Standards (NBPTS) began working together to create an advanced credential for school counselors that would tie school counseling standards to the NBPTS requirements. Negotiations ended unsuccessfully in 2003 when NBCC would not agree to (a) an advanced counselor credential controlled by a sixty-three–member board of teachers with only one school counselor representative, (b) an advanced counselor credential that does not require a master's degree, and (c) an advanced school counseling credential that is not a collaborative effort with all professional associations, accreditation, and certification organizations in counseling.

The CACREP, NBCC, and ASCA promote counselor identity. The NBPTS promotes the school counselor as educator. This text promotes the school counselor as both (see chapter 3), making failed efforts between NBCC and NBPTS disappointing in that one unified advanced credential for school counselors that promotes the school counselor's professional identity as both an educator and counselor is compatible with the new paradigm and new vision for school counseling.

The new vision school counselor focuses on academic achievement, but in relation to the provision of sound mental health–related services. Educators understand the priorities—student safety first—always. Counselor educators, parents, teachers, and school administrators desire instructional competence in a school counselor, but need clinical counseling competence in a school counselor, who is often the only mental health professional in the school building. And, unfortunately, even with the application of a collaborative model, the only counselor a troubled child or adolescent may ever see is the school counselor.

An advanced school counselor credential that is not governed by counselors and the counseling profession, and is grounded in the core propositions of *what teachers should know and be able to do* may not inspire the public's confidence in the school counselor's clinical ability to meet the personal, social, and emotional needs of their children. This is particularly significant in a charged climate where the public's confidence in our educational system is already wavering if not waning. Parents are not only questioning the ability of public schools to successfully educate their child, but the ability of public schools to identify and effectively intervene in situations with troubled students, who threaten the safety of their child.

Thus, whether one holds the philosophy that a school counselor is a counselor placed in a school setting, or an educator who applies counseling skills, the counseling component and counselor identity must be equally advanced and empowered. As such, one credential must not be pitted against the other or supported over the other. Both credentials are valuable in establishing the school counselor's advanced knowledge and expertise as an educator and as a counselor. Currently, however, only four states provide incentives to NBCC-certified school counselors, while thirty states provide incentives for NBPTS-certified school counselors. Exclusive support for the NBPTS teacher-controlled school counseling credential may be perceived as implying a belief that instructional competence supersedes clinical and counseling competence, trumping student safety.

The U.S. House of Representatives' Committee on Appropriations voiced concern regarding the NBPTS's credentialing of school counselors, encouraging the NBPTS to retain its intended focus—to improve the skills and credentials of classroom teachers (U.S. House of Representatives Report 109-143, 2006). Acting on this concern the House Committee on Appropriations has provided more flexibility to the Department of Education with regard to the earmarking of advanced credential funding. This House committee action may open the door to school administrators and all stakeholders to advocate for the recognition of the NBCC's school counselor credential as well as the NBPTS school counselor credential when providing incentives and financial supplements for the advanced credentialing of school counselors.

American School Counselor Association National Model and Standards

The ASCA provides professional development, leadership, advocacy, research, publications, and resources to school counselors worldwide. The ASCA adopted national standards (Campbell and Dahir, 1997) and created a national model (2005) to more clearly define and unify professional identity and practices.

The national model provides a framework from which to establish accountable, comprehensive, developmental school counseling programs that align with academic achievement missions and emphasizes systems-focused service delivery.

The national model provides standards, competencies, and indicators for facilitating student development in three domains (i.e., academic, career, personal/social). The model also includes school counselor performance standards that reflect new vision roles and functions.

National School Counseling Research Center

The National School Counseling Research Center (NSCRC) is currently being developed by the ASCA and ACES to promote accountability in school counseling by (a) identifying practices that contribute to academic success, (b) communicating opportunities for research collaboration, and (c) providing reliable, valid instruments for use by counselor educators and practitioners. The center supports the critical new vision roles and functions of school counselors in promoting academic achievement and school improvement.

The Center is a clearinghouse of historical and current research regarding school counseling programs and practices. In addition to supporting accountable practices in both counselor education and practice, research made available by the center can be used for professional advocacy, programming decisions, and to inform and shape policy at the local, state, and federal levels.

ACHIEVING ACADEMIC-FOCUSED
SCHOOL COUNSELING

The ASCA and TSCI call for an alignment with academic achievement missions and programming that includes strategies to help close the achievement gap. The ASCA national model and TSCI's new vision for school counseling is supported by CACREP, professional school counseling associations, and a substantial body of research and literature. Adopting an academic-focused model for school counseling is further supported by research that links student academic success to collaborative school cultures that exude an academic emphasis (Goddard, Hoy, and Woolfolk, 2000).

Failure of the mental health model to align school counseling with the mission of schools and to demonstrate an impact on academic achievement is chronicled in professional literature and exemplified in the historical exclusion of school counselors in educational reform agendas. The direction of the profession must be reversed.

School counselors are being called upon to engage in practices that more clearly focus on academic achievement while attending to students' mental health needs through collaboration and systems-focused prevention and intervention activities. Attaching school counseling to school reform initiatives and to the educational system as a whole requires changes in counselor education, practice, and leadership, as well as practical tools and approaches.

Some counselor educators and school counseling practitioners are resisting the paradigm switch, preferring to adhere to the outdated mental health–focused model for what is likely a multitude of reasons that include a lack of motivation toward change in general. Counselor educators and practitioners, who willfully continue to embrace the traditional paradigm perpetuate *business as usual* and hamper the efforts of reform-minded leaders, condemning the profession to its superfluous position— or worse. A lack of support from school counseling professionals intent upon traditional practices, must be met by an unequivocal force—school administrators.

School Administrator and School Counselor Leadership Alliance

Clearly, professional school counseling alliances have been forged and are acting as resolute and progressive forces to switch the paradigm and reverse the direction of obsolete school counseling practices. Still, school counseling reform cannot be realized without the involvement and support of school administrators at all levels—a force that has yet to be clearly defined and fully set in motion in the movement to transform school counseling.

School boards, superintendents, and school principals determine the roles and functions of school counselors within a division. Therefore, the redesign of school counseling depends upon the acceptance, support, and collective leadership of school administrators and school counseling practitioners.

Historically, school administrators come from teacher backgrounds and receive minimal training in educational leadership programs on the perspectives of school personnel other than teachers. As such, school administrators have had limited opportunities to fully understand the roles and functions of the school counselor as delineated by the school counseling profession.

School counselors, most of whom were schooled under the traditional pedagogy and prior to the establishment of the national school counseling standards and the ASCA national model, are also unable to clearly articulate their professional roles, functions, identity, direction for change, and goals related to academic achievement. As a result, school administrators have been relegated to the position of spectator, despite supervisory responsibilities and a vested interest in integrating this disconnected and specialized subset into the educational system.

Therefore, the first barrier to overcome in establishing a school counselor and school administrator alliance is a mutual understanding of the independent and interdependent functions of each of the system's components. Appreciating this interconnectedness, changes that affect one component have consequences for the whole, making the transformation of school counseling a pipe dream without the absolute approval and involvement of school administrators. Fittingly, the systems-integration philosophies of W. Edwards Deming have been likened to the contemporary leadership role of school administrators.

> Systems thinking is like conducting a piece of music for an orchestra. . . . [E]ach element can function apart from the others. . . . [T]he flute solo may be pleasant, the percussion powerful, the strings, in perfect harmony . . . it is the work of the conductor who pulls all the parts together into one beautiful song. Only then do the musicians—and the audience members—get the full and intended effect. When the parts are working together as a thriving whole under the direction of a skilled school leader, the district becomes more effective. (Sutton, 2006, p. 47)

School administrators are being challenged to ensure a standards-based curriculum, heighten accountability, and integrate specialized resources and manpower to bring about monumental systemic change in education. School counselors are being called upon to engage their specialized skills in counseling and education and to connect to the system in order to align with school missions and to directly impact global student achievement using accountable practices. For the first time in history, school administrator and school counselor paradigms, perspectives, and goals are homogenous, making leadership alliances not only possible, but probable and uniquely powerful.

SUMMARY

In order to survive as a profession and to meet the diverse needs of students in today's educational climate, school counselor education and

practice must switch paradigms from the traditional mental health–
focused model that serves a selected few to the new academic-focused
paradigm that serves the many and aligns with the academic achievement mission of schools. Despite support for the new paradigm from
the major forces that shape the profession of school counseling, some
counselor educators and practitioners are content to continue promoting
the outdated, failed mental health model, heightening the need for the
leadership of reform-minded school administrators, who can ensure the
implementation of the new paradigm.

The new vision model promotes needs-driven, standards-based, accountable programming that aligns school counseling with academic
achievement missions and contributes to closing the achievement gap.
An immediate need exists for school counselor and school administrator partnerships and for academic-focused approaches and electronic
data reporting tools to implement change on a systems level.

2

Meeting Stakeholder Needs

The school counseling program does not belong to the school counselor; it belongs to the stakeholders. New vision school counseling programs meet the needs of the system vs. the needs of the selected few. However, the prevalence of primarily individual-focused interventions implies a need for school counselors to develop a deeper understanding of systems-focused programming that is driven by the stakeholder collective.

Collaboration and consultation with stakeholders, namely school administrators, parents, and teachers, are essential to developing a customized school counseling program that meets the unique needs of diverse students and the total school environment. The ASCA recommends establishing an advisory council in which stakeholder membership is representative of the community's diversity. The ASCA national model (2005) provides guidelines for creating a viable school counseling advisory council that promotes a systems perspective.

The AASA Center for System Leadership (www.oasa.org), although designed to assist district level leaders in using systems thinking to shape education and achieve universal student success, is a viable resource for school counselors and school counseling supervisors. The center assists educators' efforts to "build and sustain capacity for change, provide leadership in a diverse and highly political environment, work within the present system while leading the change process, and bring local leaders and stakeholders together to support the school system" (Sutton, 2006, p. 47).

The continuous involvement of stakeholders is key to obtaining correct information and identifying systemic needs, which are vital to meaningful comprehensive school counseling program planning. Identifying stake-holder needs requires knowledge of existing relevant data sources, partic-ularly those within the school and division. In addition, school counselors must acquire the necessary skills to conduct meaningful needs assess-ments.

DATA-DRIVEN PROGRAM PLANNING

The ASCA and the TSCI, as well as NCLB, call upon school counselors to use data in order to make informed decisions that positively effect universal academic achievement. Data-based decisions drive school counseling program practices and the application of school counseling developmental standards.

The study of data is a powerful process that can reveal stakeholder needs, inequities and barriers to academic achievement, and other infor-mation essential to targeted, goal-focused programming and practices. The evolving nature of data collection and sharing often reveals addi-tional sources of data and which sources of data are the most useful.

School counselors, who make use of the robust sources of data on hand, have a foundation for accountable program production. The fol-lowing list includes possible data sources generally available to school counselors for needs identification and program evaluation.

Academic Portfolio Goals Completion
Attendance Rates
Career and Technical Education Program Participation
Career Assessments
Career Portfolio–Career Action Plan Goal Completion
Classroom Performance Data
College Acceptance Rates
Conflict Resolution/Peer Mediation Records
Consultation
Course Enrollment Patterns
Demographic Data
Discipline Records
Drop-out Rates
Expulsion Records

Financial Data
Grade Reports
Graduation Rates
Homework Completion Records
Industry Certification Participation/Pass Rates
Interest Inventories
Needs Assessment
Nontraditional Program Track (GED, Job Corps, etc.)
Parent/Community School Involvement–Volunteer Data
Parent-Teacher Conference Records
Pre-Post-program Knowledge/Skills Measure
Promotion and Retention Rates
PTA/PTSA Attendance Rates
Scholarship Records
School Event Attendance Rates
Scores on the GED Official Practice Test
Self-Assessment
Standardized Assessment Data
Student Community Service/Volunteer Data
Suspensions (in-school)
Suspensions (out-of-school)
Time-out Records

It is prudent to capture data from multiple sources in order to enhance the quality of program planning. Multiple data sources assist school counselors in clarifying need and identifying levels of need for timely, successful programming.

School counselors can leverage the power of information technology to mine the seemingly unlimited amounts of information for data-driven program planning that can be used to inform and improve educational practices. Data-based decision making in education has been defined as the "process of collecting, analyzing, reporting, and using data for school improvement" (Poynton and Carey, 2006, p. 121).

Many data-based decision making models are available for school counselors to use as a framework for facilitating the process. Poynton and Carey (2006) provide school counselors with a review of data-based decision making models both within and outside of school counseling. These models share a belief in the importance of stakeholder inclusion in the programming process and assume a collaborative climate. While this assumption is valid in some school communities, it cannot be assumed in all communities. School data and data generated from needs assessments can assist in assessing school-community climate.

School personnel and parent-community relationships have been adversarial in some districts. Educators often blame cultural differences, diverging values, a lack of parental involvement, and family dysfunction for poor academic achievement. On the other hand, parents tend to blame discrimination, inattentiveness, and a lack of concern by school personnel for poor academic achievement.

School administrators across the nation have made tremendous progress in improving parent-community and school personnel relations through the AASA *Stand Up for Public Education* call to action. The AASA call to action exposes public education as the "heart of our democracy" (Gee, 2005, p. 44). AASA has united with stakeholders to provide the highest quality education to our most valuable resource—the child.

In settings where adversarial relationships exist between school personnel and parents, school counselors can lead by AASA's example. Like school administrators, school counselors can engage interpersonal, collaborative, and communication skills to impart information and remove the barriers that impede cooperative and productive partnerships with a child's most valuable educational resource—the parent.

Conducting Needs Assessments

Needs assessments are an excellent and time-honored means by which school counselors can identify and target relevant needs for appropriate programming. Conducting needs assessments involves collecting and analyzing information regarding the needs of the stakeholders.

Assessments can be written or oral, conducted in person, on the telephone, and via the Internet or by mail. Needs can be assessed using a selection of participants from the population to be served, the entire population to be served, or by using focus groups, community forums, and/or key informants.

School counselors who elect to use focus groups select several individuals representative of the population to be served. Collectively, needs are discussed openly, prioritized, and documented. The school counselor generally guides the process with a structured or semistructured format.

Community forums have merit in that any stakeholder wishing to be involved may participate. School counselors announce the community forum meeting and the topic of discussion. It may be necessary to divide large groups into smaller subgroups during initial needs identification discussions. Each subgroup selects one member to serve as purveyor of group needs during collective discussions in order to maintain orderly communications. The school counselor provides each group with one written needs assessment to be completed before initiating the collective community forum discussion. The school counselor leads the collective discussion anticipating precipitating debate between subgroups, particularly with regard to the levels of importance placed on needs.

Key informants are useful and may be surveyed individually or in small groups. Key informants are selected based on their vast knowledge of the population to be served but may not necessarily be a member of the population.

Initial needs assessments for administration to adult stakeholders might begin with general questions. Responses to the initial questions may suggest a need for more specific follow-up questions vital to targeted, needs-driven programming and identifying best practices. General questions might include the following:

- What school counseling services do you find helpful?
- What additional school counseling services would you find helpful?
- What are the strengths of the school counseling program?
- What suggestions do you have for possible improvements to the school counseling program?
- What would be your suggestions for improvement?
- What questions do you have regarding the school counseling program and services?
- What are some ways you would like to become involved in the school counseling program?
- What barriers to student development have you observed or do you believe exist in our school?
- What suggestions do you have for the school counseling program for removing such barriers?

Needs assessments for children may be read aloud with interpretations dependent upon developmental level. Needs assessments that make use of the check system are ideal for children and special-needs populations. For example, simply list the topics and have students place a check in the box beside the topic(s) of interest:

☐ Dealing with Bullies
☐ Safety (+ Internet Safety)
☐ Nutrition and Health
☐ Study Skills and Organization
☐ Test Taking Skills
☐ Making and Keeping Friends
☐ Self-Control
☐ Managing Time
☐ Managing Anger
☐ Communication
☐ Career
☐ Conflict Resolution/Peer Mediation (Getting Along)
☐ Problem Solving
☐ Decision Making (Making Good Choices)
☐ Self-Esteem (Liking Myself)
☐ Managing Stress (Expressing Feelings)
☐ Setting and Achieving Goals

The check system also allows for ease of administration. The school counselor may find it useful to combine elements of both structures based on intended purpose and population.

RESEARCH-SUPPORTED CURRICULUM DEVELOPMENT

School improvement agendas and new vision practices for school counselors call for the use of standards-based programming and research-supported interventions, necessitating that educators and school counselors become savvy consumers of research. Standards-based programming is the focus of the next chapter.

Research-supported practices require familiarity with professional, peer-reviewed education and counseling journals and the ability to identify important components of relevant studies. Simpson, LaCava, and Graner (2004) recommend focusing on the theoretical/scientific base, the target population, outcomes, and resources needed to implement and possibly replicate the method.

The ACA has a list of counseling related peer-reviewed journals on their Web site at www.counselor.com. The Center for School Counseling Outcome Research (CSCOR), which houses the National Panel for School Counseling Evidence-Based Practice, has a Web site dedicated to research-supported practices and issues of accountability for school counselors at www.cscor.org. The National Technology Institute for School Counselors at www.techcounselor.org houses research-supported information and resources. Also forthcoming is the ASCA National School Counseling Research Center (NSCRC), discussed in chapter 1, which disseminates information for the facilitation of school counseling accountability and academic success for all students.

School counselors who have evaluated their own programs and activities may use those findings to support subsequent programming and the continuous improvement of practices. Chapter 4 discusses the benefits of practitioner program evaluation in greater detail.

Once the school counselor has an understanding of systemic programming based on stakeholder needs, those needs are translated into measurable goals and research-supported curriculum activities, and interventions are identified to achieve specific student competencies. For example, consider the concept of self-esteem hypothetically identified as a topic of interest on the needs assessment completed by students in your school. In addition to identification on the needs assessment, the school counselor demonstrates and documents how self-esteem impacts academic achievement. The school counselor also explores research-supported programs and interventions aimed at building self-esteem in order to develop an evidence-based curriculum.

For example, the school counselor seeks to answer the following questions: Does a correlation exist between self-esteem and academic performance? What does the research say about the academic proficiency of students who have a negative self-esteem versus those who have a positive self-esteem? Is poor self-esteem considered a barrier to academic achievement? If so, would it be logical to conclude that programs that enhance self-esteem remove a barrier to academic achievement? Which counseling and instructional interventions have been used in the past with positive outcomes? With what populations were the counseling and instructional interventions successful?

Once programming need and how it relates to academic achievement has been established, research-supported counseling approaches, techniques, and activities for enhancing self-esteem are identified, as well as the school counseling standards and student competencies for developing the program curriculum. The new vision school counselor has now established a data-driven, research-supported program that meets the needs of stakeholders. However, while the program, like traditional school counseling programming, demonstrates a direct impact on personal/social development, the program is designed in such a way as to imply an indirect impact on academic achievement.

The new vision school counselor cannot be content with an indirect or implied impact on academic achievement. New vision school counselors develop programs that establish a direct impact on academic achievement. The next chapter introduces standards blending as a means to this end.

SUMMARY

The school counseling program belongs to the stakeholders. The school counselor actively seeks to identify stakeholder needs using data analysis and data collection to include needs assessment techniques.

A multitude of potential data sources are available for assessing stakeholder need. Needs assessments aid school counselors in targeting and prioritizing programming, and can be accomplished in a variety of ways.

Accountable practices necessitate that school counselors become savvy consumers of research. In order to link personal/social topics to academic achievement, school counselors explore, identify, and apply research-supported interventions.

3

The Fabric of Reform: Conceptualizing and Operationalizing School Counselor Roles

The ASCA, in collaboration with the CACREP, the TSCI, and professional counseling associations, has made great strides in defining contemporary school counseling functions, services, and practices. However, vague school counselor roles and a blurring between roles and functions continue to strangle the profession's progress.

Lieberman (2004) presents a plethora of research and literature that consistently faults role ambiguity and the profession's inability to establish consistent school counselor roles for the historical struggles of school counseling. In the present, an inability to agree upon, conceptualize, and operationalize the roles of the school counselor threatens the success of the profession's new vision.

Some believe that by accommodating the new vision's academic-focused paradigm, they are neglecting the mental health role of the school counselor (Guerra, 1998). The mighty reaction that resonated within the profession implied that the switch to an academic-focused paradigm equated to a change in professional identity—a change that some fear will result in a unilateral identification of the school counselor as educator vs. counselor.

School counselors are clinically-trained mental health providers with specialized training in child and adolescent development and education. One constant within and outside of contemporary school counseling is the recognition that school counselors perform functions that are indicative of both counselors and educators.

This text promotes the dual roles of educator and counselor providing a conceptualization and operationalization of these roles in the context of the new vision's academic-focused paradigm. Defining and framing school counselor functions in relation to these dual roles provides a conceptually sound structure from which to operationalize and authenticate the roles of the new school counselor. Conceptualization of the dual roles of the new vision school counselor can be summarized as follows: *school counselors are both mental health specialists and educational specialists in a school setting who focus on the student as a learner, with school counseling services designed, delivered, and documented in an accountable manner that directly and indirectly advances academic achievement, enhances student development and well-being, and informs important others.*

New vision school counselors integrate the dual roles of educational and mental health specialist into a succinct guiding philosophy that drives the affective and cognitive domains of programming and professional practices. The philosophy can be encapsulated as follows: *a healthy mind is an educable mind and a healthy mind is not defined as free from physical, mental, emotional, social, and environmental distress.* The fabric of reform rests in the school counselor's ability to embrace this belief and to integrate skills as educational specialists and mental health specialists to meet the academic, career, and personal/social development needs of today's diverse youth.

The adept new vision school counselor moves fluently between the two domains for optimal student development. Sustaining this noble philosophy are accountable practices that demonstrate the direct impact of comprehensive school counseling programs on student academic achievement and total student development on a systems level.

As mental health specialists and educational specialists, new vision school counselors engage in shared functions. These functions include the following: teaming, consulting, informing, collaborating, leading, advocating, counseling, programming, assessing, referring, evaluating, coordinating, and reporting.

The remainder of this chapter is dedicated to operationalizing the school counselor's dual roles. In doing so, the specific new vision functions and activities inherent in each unique role are delineated.

SCHOOL COUNSELOR: THE ROLE OF MENTAL HEALTH SPECIALIST

CACREP ensures the clinical competence of school counselors for the role of mental health specialist by ensuring successful articulation through core counseling areas that include the following: professional identity; social and cultural diversity; human growth and development; career development; helping relationships; group work; assessment; and research and program evaluation.

The new vision school counselor as educational specialist, while focused on promoting academic achievement, has a distinct, but mutually supporting role as mental health specialist. Thus, school counselors practicing from the new vision paradigm do not abandon the mental health needs of students. Likewise, school counselors practicing from the new paradigm do not abandon the academic needs of students who are experiencing personal, social, physical, environmental, and behavioral challenges. School counselors who believe it is futile to address the academic needs of students in the midst of mental health–related difficulties are likely perpetuating achievement gaps and inequitable access to educational opportunities. The fruits of academic-focused school counseling are enjoyed by all students. The academic-focused mental health specialist fully understands how personal, social, and emotional development affects learning and designs prevention and intervention programs accordingly.

New vision school counselors, like traditional school counselors, are steadfast in addressing the individual mental health needs of students. Individual counseling is a core delivery component of a comprehensive school counseling program. However, the traditional mental health model has created an overreliance on individual counseling. An overreliance on individual counseling is inadequate and unjustifiable in today's systems-focused educational climate.

> Mental health models conceptualize social-emotional functioning as ends in themselves. This explains in part why some K–12 students are in individual school counseling "forever" and why school counseling goals from a mental health perspective are vague and tangential to an academic success and learning focus. (Eschenauer and Hayes, 2005, p. 245)

The new paradigm for school counseling emphasizes collaboration, underscoring the need to make appropriate counseling referrals to meet the complex mental health needs of students. School counselors can help to reduce and even prevent the horrific acts of school violence demonstrated at Columbine, Virginia Tech, and other schools across the nation by remaining diligent in their efforts to identify and encourage familial support and make appropriate referrals for troubled students.

School counselors "tend to conceptualize solutions in terms of what they know how to do instead of what is really required in the given situation" (Eschenauer and Hayes, 2005, p. 245). For that reason, school counseling alone is not in the best interest of children and adolescents experiencing severe, persistent, and progressive issues. Additionally, to provide ongoing counseling sessions with students whose issues cannot be sufficiently addressed within the scope of school counseling and within the expertise of the school counselor is in violation of professional ethical guidelines. School counselors can best meet the specific mental health needs of these students through a collaborative model.

New vision school counselors work with parents or child protective services, as deemed appropriate, and other professionals within and outside of the school system to provide optimal services that place the safety and well-being of children first. School counselors may involve the school psychologist, school social worker, child study team, and special education teachers. School counselors may provide parents with community resources that include specialized counselors, psychological and psychiatric services, social services, child care services, community services boards, and support groups.

Research has indicated that school counselor collaboration with outside agencies, namely community mental health agencies, is a growing trend in today's schools (Hobbs and Collison, 1995). Thus, conditions are ripe for the switch to a paradigm that emphasizes a collaborative approach to meeting the mental health needs of students. Based on their investigation, Hobbs and Collison encourage school counselors to keep in mind that the success of a collaborative model is largely dependent upon school administrator support and assistance in resolving logistical issues.

Once appropriate referrals are in place, school counselors can implement brief interventions and consult with teachers and parents to provide strategies for implementation at home and in the classroom. Interventions may include fostering optimism, cognitive restructuring, problem solving, and goal setting. School counselors assist students in identifying support systems, unique personal strengths, and information to strengthen protective factors and enhance resilience. Developing students' resilience enables them to overcome threats to educational success and to successfully engage life's challenges. Interventions that place responsibility for success within the student are educational, empowering, and help develop coping skills that can be accessed into adulthood.

The relationship between academic success and personal, emotional, social, and physical well-being is a door that swings both ways. As such, it is important for school counselors to encourage students faced with mental health–related issues and physical challenges to believe in their ability to change, grow, and overcome challenges. School counselors encourage impaired students to embrace academics as an avenue to a promising, self-directed future. Academic-focused channeling can be therapeutic, motivational, and build competencies, self-esteem, and psychological resilience—epitomizing the specialty of school counseling. Challenge can be our greatest asset, pushing us onward and upward. Standards blending, discussed later in this chapter, exploits this reciprocal relationship for total student development.

In addition to intervention, new vision school counselors demonstrate a heightened emphasis on being proactive in anticipating and meeting the mental health needs of all students. Therefore, in addition to programs and lessons designed to meet the unique needs of a school population or specific classroom, new vision school counselors engage in purposeful programming designed to remove formidable personal, social, and emotional barriers to academic achievement.

Chapter 4 provides an effective example of a schoolwide peer mediation program and evaluation that identifies, targets, and reduces school violence, an obstacle to academic achievement and the personal, social, and emotional well-being of students (Schellenberg, Parks-Savage, and Rehfuss, 2007). The program studied establishes the need for schoolwide peer mediation programs and reveals the link between peer mediation programs and academic achievement. The study documents research and literature that emphasize the detrimental effects of aggressive student interactions on the school's culture, learning environment, and academic productivity.

Proactive approaches to meeting the needs of students may require that school counselors position themselves in ways that increase visibility, which aids in enhancing school climate; fostering relationships with students, parents, teachers, and principals; and identifying *at risk* students (i.e., withdrawn, flat affect, socially inept, overly aggressive, visibly distressed). For example, school counselors may greet students in main hallways prior to the start of morning classes and at the end of the school day. School counselors might consider frequent visits to the cafeteria to give out bookmarks that contain useful information such as study and test-taking tips, important dates, names of school counselors, counseling department services and Web site, and career exploration resources and access codes. In addition, promoting the *open door* policy, conveying an approachable demeanor, and maintaining a welcoming office (e.g., chair facing the door vs. back to the door) encourages interaction.

Many adults and students who experience distress do not actively seek out support (Auger, 2004). In addition, many stakeholders simply cannot find the time to make an appointment to meet with the school counselor. As such, it is important that school counselors be creative in getting meaningful information to stakeholders for sound decision making and problem solving. Information and resources might include: crises response; support programs; parenting programs; tutoring contacts; substance use/abuse; eating disorders; counseling services available to students; study skills; test-taking strategies; organizational and time management skills; problem solving and conflict resolution; communication skills; and information that describes what to look for in determining the need for counseling services.

Establishing or tapping into a school-based Parent-Teacher-Student Resource Center (PTSRC) as an avenue for information dissemination is essential to meeting the needs of all stakeholders. PTSRCs are efficient mediums for promoting student development in a way that accommodates diverse schedules. The PTSRC is also an excellent way to get parents involved.

As Moles (1993) pointed out, there are many parents who want very much to get involved in the local school community but for a variety of reasons do not step forward. Extend an invitation to parents and be specific about the assistance and hours for which they are being recruited—watch what happens!

Parent volunteers are often an untapped resource in schools where human resources are generally limited. Parent volunteers can oversee daily PTSRC operations, providing assistance and direction to stakeholders seeking specific information, coordinating requests for information, and maintaining informational flow.

Web sites are another cost-effective and efficient medium for making resources available to stakeholders. Web sites communicate information in a broad and expedient manner so as to meet the immediate needs of stakeholders. Information and resources listed on school counseling Web sites can enhance student development and well-being and support healthy schools, homes, and communities.

New vision school counselors are dogmatic in their efforts to meet the mental health needs of students. In applying the constructs of the new paradigm, school counselors do not neglect the mental health needs of students, but expand services and promote a more proactive and collaborative approach to meeting students' personal, social, emotional, and physical needs. Practicing under the new paradigm requires school counselors to exercise their mental health specialist role in relation to fulfilling their educational specialist role—the role that sets counseling in the schools apart from other counseling specialties and defines our profession.

SCHOOL COUNSELOR: THE ROLE OF EDUCATIONAL SPECIALIST

Education and training that distinguishes the school counselor as an educational specialist includes: pre-K–12 program design and delivery; classroom instruction; theories of learning; child and adolescent development; standardized testing and assessment; use of technology; behavioral theory; disability and exceptional behavior; identification of student competencies and ways to achieve academic competency; identification and removal of barriers to academic achievement; developing effective learning environments; needs assessment; and educational program evaluation. New vision school counselors work closely with stakeholders, namely teachers, engaging their skills as educational specialists to provide the finest services to students and parents and to accomplish the academic mission of schools.

Because fulfillment of the role of educational specialist involves instruction, a few states still require a teaching background in order to become a school counselor. Therefore, it is important that this text speak to the research in this area of continued debate, which has recently been aroused with the NBPTS's establishment of an advanced voluntary certification for school counselors (discussed in chapter 1).

Decades of research have examined the question of whether or not school counselors should be teachers prior to becoming school counselors.

Results of these studies indicate that school administrators and school counselor supervisors deem school counselors without teaching experience to be as effective as those with teaching experience. Unexpectedly, in some cases the majority of school counselors without teaching experience were found to be more effective in their overall performance than those with teaching experience (Beale, 1995; Dilley, Foster, and Bowers, 1973; Olson and Allen, 1993).

One landmark study conducted by Arbuckle (1961) during the crux of the debate provides evidence that having served as a teacher results in a multitude of poor counseling habits. The implications of this study are significant, indicating a need for counselor educators to work closely with former teachers to extinguish most of what they had learned as teachers in order to become effective school counselors.

Arbuckle's (1961) findings are further supported in a more recent study of the personal and professional adjustments of school counseling interns with and without teaching experience. The study conducted by Peterson, et al. (2004) indicated that former teachers faced unique challenges that threatened their successful transition into the school counseling profession. Again, these findings indicate the need for counselor educators to more closely monitor the personal and professional adjustment of former teachers vs. that of students with no teaching background.

Although it has been established that teaching experience does not equal effective school counseling, there is general agreement that instructional skills are helpful in a profession that is expected to provide instruction. Therefore, counselor educators are diligent in their efforts to ensure the instructional competency of pre-service school counselors in course curriculum and in the practice setting during counselor education programs.

In addition to the formal course work noted earlier in this chapter, counselor educators require demonstration of instructional competencies with diverse populations during classroom experiential learning activities and internships. Also, pre-service school counselors are required to demonstrate knowledge of the pre-K–12 curriculum and engage in practicum and internship experiences throughout the counselor education program. Therefore, pre-service school counselors have multiple opportunities to enhance their knowledge of curriculum development, collaborate with teachers, and to develop classroom management and instructional skills while also gaining a familiarity with the school setting.

Counselor education programs clearly prepare school counselors for their role as educational specialists. Nonetheless the new paradigm's heightened emphasis on aligning school counseling activities with academic achievement accentuates the need to optimize the instructional competency of school counselors. Therefore, supplementary school counselor training is suggested in instructional strategies, academic achievement, learning theory, and multiple intelligences.

School counselors can increase their skills in these areas by taking related education courses as electives during their counselor education programs. School counselors might also consider engaging in self-initiated learning such as job shadowing, interviewing, and dialoguing with currently practicing teachers and principals. Participating in instructional planning and related conferences and workshops and writing and reviewing journal articles are additional ways in which school counselors can build instructional competencies.

Instruction is but one function inherent in the school counselor's role of educational specialist. School counselors as educational specialists are also required to: apply academic standards; interpret standardized testing score reports; engage in standardized testing programs; develop research-supported curriculum; and create and evaluate needs-based educational programs. School counselors as educational specialists also work with teachers to modify the classroom climate for optimal learning and to develop academic contracts and schedules of reinforcement.

School counselors join hands with teachers and administrators to identify systemic areas of academic deficits and specific low-achieving student populations. School counselors tailor programming to target academic needs while simultaneously meeting the personal, social, and career development needs of students. School counselors identify the divergent needs of each grade level, each classroom, and specific students, to direct classroom guidance and small group interventions.

STANDARDS BLENDING: ALIGNING SCHOOL COUNSELING WITH ACADEMIC ACHIEVEMENT

Leaders in education and school counseling agree that implementation of standards-based programs that align school counseling with academic achievement missions are *best practices* for new vision school counselors. A redefinition of best practices prompted by the contemporary school reform movement and the TSCI has created a need to explicitly align school counseling with the mission of schools. Alignment approaches are needed that provide school counselors with a direct path for increasing academic achievement and closing the achievement gap.

To date, alignment approaches that integrate academic standards and school counseling standards have been random, spur-of-the-moment, superfluous, and/or absent from school counseling programming. This chapter introduces standards blending as a specific and unified approach for inclusion as a deliberate, inveterate, and integral component of a comprehensive school counseling program. The paragraphs that follow demonstrate how standards blending can be implemented and assimilated as a permanent programming strategy for universal academic achievement.

Standards blending is a systems-focused, integrative, and student-centered approach that directly and overtly aligns school counseling programs with academic achievement missions. School counselors methodically identify and blend specific core academic standards with school counseling standards for integrated lessons that assist students in making connections to real life and across curricula. As a primary and anchored appendage to a comprehensive developmental school counseling program, standards blending is the embodiment of the academic- and systems-focused paradigm.

Standards blending does not replace the mental health role of the school counselor nor was it meant as an approach to address every unique issue within a school. The approach requires the school counselor to make use of their skills as both educational and mental health specialist, integrating school counseling and core academic standards in order to meet both the mental health needs and educational needs of students simultaneously.

School counselors may wish to blend all core academic standards with the school counseling standards to create the alignment. However, it is recommended that language arts and mathematics standards be the focus of standards blending because *reading, writing,* and *arithmetic* have always been basic to schooling and to building a solid foundation from which to learn other core subjects.

In addition, reinforcing language arts and mathematics standards assists schools in meeting the goal of reading and math proficiency by the

2013–2014 school year as set forth by NCLB, and thereby the professional leadership of school counselors and administrators. The national mathematics standards (NCTM, 2000), standards for the English language arts (NCTE, 1996), and the national school counseling standards (Campbell and Dahir, 1997) were also selected because individual states use these standards to create more specific local standards, making them applicable to educators across the nation.

The unrelenting call for accountability in educational practices and standards-based educational reform, namely NCLB, has heightened the importance of rigorous standards and research-based practices by underscoring their importance in establishing evidence-based practices. Standards blending is grounded in these nationally accepted standards that are influenced by research and knowledge in the field.

In addition to a rigorous standards base, impact data collected to assess the meaningfulness of the standards blending approach is promising. Preliminary data indicate that standards blending reinforces the academic standards that have already been covered by classroom teachers, while teaching new information and concepts embodied in the academic, personal/social, and career development domains of the national school counseling standards.

The recent study involving 103 public school second grade students in five classrooms consisting of both general education and special-needs students resulted in knowledge development for minority and nonminority participants on both the school counseling and academic curriculum components (Schellenberg, 2007). The program evaluation also found all knowledge gains to be statistically significant. Details of the standards-blended program and evaluation are documented in operational plans and results reports in chapter 5, using an electronic school counseling data reporting system designed by a school counselor for school counselors.

As an integrative, student-centered approach to learning, standards blending encourages students to draw upon previous knowledge, make connections, get involved, explore, discuss, discover, and personalize the content. Standards blending promotes the application of differential instruction, assessing student needs, accommodating unique student learning profiles, and considering student readiness and interests in curriculum planning and delivery.

In addition, standards blending promotes the multiple learning categories (i.e., cognitive, affective, and psychomotor) and six learning levels of Bloom's Taxonomy (Bloom, 1953; i.e., knowledge, comprehension, application, analysis, synthesis, evaluation). As a holistic and constructivist approach, standards blending is an instructional strategy that is compatible with brain-based learning.

Standards blending is a pragmatic, theoretically sound, and potentially powerful approach that provides students with a method by which to improve comprehension by connecting curricula and visualizing the interrelationships of learning and real life. Students are provided the opportunity to socially interact with the curriculum, fellow students, and teachers in small learning communities where information is processed and problems are examined, deconstructed, and resolved. Approaches such as these have been linked to the development of background knowledge, intrinsic interest, and higher-order intelligence, as well as greater academic achievement and a heightened motivation toward learning (Marzano, 2004; Sink, 2005; Vansteenkiste, Lens, and Deci, 2006).

Blending academic standards and school counseling standards requires a working knowledge of school counseling and academic standards and consultation with the classroom teacher to coordinate the pacing of lessons. Most schools offer pacing guides which outline the timing of classroom instruction that addresses specific academic standards. This chapter provides school administrators, counselor educators, and school counseling practitioners with an understanding of, and practical applications for, blending national standards, state standards, or both with school counseling standards at the state and national level.

Standards blending can be delivered as a systems support mechanism using schoolwide classroom guidance curriculum and as a responsive services strategy using small groups and individual counseling as recommended by the ASCA and AASA. School counselors select which language arts and mathematics standards to blend based on instructional pacing guides, consultation with teachers, and as identified by an examination of standardized test scores, state and classroom assessment data, and/or other student performance data.

Consider the following case for illustration of a classroom or small group standards-blended lesson. The lesson blends both eighth grade national school counseling standards and national mathematics and language arts core academic standards. Also, note the differential instructional components in the lesson's design and activities and the inclusion of the three domains and six levels of learning of Bloom's Taxonomy.

The school counselor is preparing to conduct eighth grade classroom guidance lessons and/or small groups addressing the school counseling standards and student competencies for career development as deemed appropriate to a comprehensive school counseling program and as indicated by a needs assessment conducted at the start of the school year. The school's academic pacing guide or eighth grade teacher indicates that the eighth grade English teachers are working on oral language development with the students in March, specifically interviewing techniques to gain information—or this was identified as a need for a specific group of students in which case small group counseling may be conducted.

In addition to school counseling standards and competencies, the school counselor incorporates the language arts standards being addressed at that time. The standards-blended lesson curriculum includes a discussion of the importance of researching different careers to locate, evaluate, and interpret career and educational information (school counseling career development competency). Informational interviews are defined and discussed to include students' thoughts and feelings associated with the career exploration process and conducting informational interviews. Students are asked to give examples of the value and different uses of informational interviews and how they compare to other methods used in the past for the collection of information. Students are asked to conduct an informational interview (language arts competency) for the purpose of career exploration (school counseling competency). Individually, students prepare ten relevant questions for the interview (language arts competency). Students role-play the interview with the school counselor and each other, asking the questions they prepared (language arts competency) and noting the responses (language arts competency). Together the class evaluates the effectiveness of the interviews in learning more about career choices (language arts and school counseling competencies).

Math standards being addressed by teachers at the present time include estimations, data analysis and conjectures, and identifying the mean of a data set. Therefore, the school counselor requires that at least five questions involve proportions such as scaling questions (e.g., how would you rate your job satisfaction on a scale of 1 to 10?). Students are then required to represent scaled responses using a table or graph, and then analyze patterns, relationships, and similarities within their

*data set and differences between each other's data sets. Together the
group develops inferences about their findings (language arts, mathematics, and school counseling competencies).*

*The school counselor closes the lesson with an appraisal of the in-
formational interview specific to career exploration. Students also
judge the applicability and usefulness of informational interviews in
other areas of their personal, academic, and professional lives. Again,
the school counselor assesses students' thoughts and feelings associated
with the career exploration process and conducting informational interviews.*

The eighth grade standards-blended lesson noted above can also be tai-
lored to meet the developmental and educational needs of high school
students. This classroom guidance lesson or small group activity applied to ninth, tenth, eleventh, and twelfth grade students meets school
counseling career development standards as well as language arts (e.g.,
communication skills and strategies, evaluating data, developing research skills, application of language skills) and mathematics standards
(e.g., number and operations, measurement, data analysis and probability, developing and evaluating inferences and predictions based on data,
mathematical communication, connections, and representation).

Closing the Achievement Gap with Standards Blending

School counselors must take on leadership functions in school reform
in order to attach professional practices to academic achievement missions and transform school counseling. Current educational reform initiatives require educators to disaggregate data and identify existing subgroup discrepancies in areas related to student academic achievement.
Educators are then challenged to design approaches that assist in closing such gaps in order to demonstrate adequate yearly progress.

National data have identified academic achievement gaps between
low-income and minority students and their more affluent peers, students
with disabilities and nondisabled students, and between males and fe-
males. Therefore, once school counselors, in collaboration with school
administrators and teachers, have identified low-achieving subgroups in
a particular school/district, research-supported and standards-based programming should be designed to aid in closing achievement gaps.

New vision school counselors are demonstrating a direct impact on closing the achievement gap when students who are considered part of the gap participate in standards-blended programs that result in increased academic achievement. For example, once identified, school counselors can design small group curriculum to specifically target areas of academic weaknesses. While strengthening areas of academic deficits, school counselors simultaneously address personal, social, academic, and career related issues using standards blending. These issues may be identified by research as generally problematic, that is, causing or correlating with poor academic achievement, or by teachers, students, and parents as an identified need (i.e., self-esteem, social skills, problem solving, test-taking anxiety). Identification of need by research and stakeholder is a powerful union for programming support.

Low-achieving students often experience multiple precipitating issues and stressors that frequently go unrecognized and untreated, placing these students at risk for school failure. Using standards-blended programs, school counselors can address the mental health needs of these students, building personal, social, and emotional well-being and resilience, while simultaneously and directly addressing targeted academic needs.

For example, several students are referred to the school counselor due to personal, social, and behavioral issues. The school counselor, through consultation with the teacher(s) and/or a review of student records/data, finds that some of the students are also having difficulty in mastering specific academic standards. Investigation also reveals that the students are considered to be in the achievement gap population. Although the school counselor could blend the core academic standards currently being addressed in the classroom, standards blending becomes a more powerful and precise technique for closing achievement gaps when programming specifically targets students in the gap in areas of academic weakness.

Consider the following standards-blended lesson for illustration of a small group that provides students with both remediation and reinforcement in language arts and mathematics in addition to social skills development. Again, note in the lesson's design differential instruction strategies, and the inclusion of Bloom's three domains and six levels of learning.

A teacher refers Topeka, a third grade student, to the school counselor for a social skills small group intervention. Consultation with the teacher and a review of Topeka's class work and formal assessments reveal difficulty in math, particularly with number and number sense such as the concepts of greater than, less than, and equal to; parts of sets; and fractions. As a result of school counselor-teacher consultation, while defining, identifying, experiencing, and appraising the concepts of sharing and fairness in the social skills group using role plays and social skills scenarios (language arts and school counseling competencies), the school counselor also addresses areas of weaknesses in mathematics.

The school counselor gives Topeka twenty social skills scenario cards and asks her to give herself and each student the same, or an equal, number of cards (mathematics competencies). After Topeka has passed out all the cards, the school counselor counts the cards in front of each of the four students and involves students in discussions that connect the concepts of sharing, fairness, sets, greater than, less than, and fractions. The cards, students, and role plays are manipulated in order to visualize the relationships, create predictions, and to assess the value of the language arts, mathematics, and social skills concepts presented.

The school counselor encourages storytelling (language arts, mathematics, and school counseling competencies) to relate learning to individual student experiences, needs, and relationships—to life—and to ensure students' understanding of the information presented. Throughout the group lessons, each student's academic areas of weakness are addressed using differential instruction based on specific core academic standards in the areas of weakness, and identified learning styles.

The standards-blended small group intervention presented above is designed to enhance total student development by targeting personal, social, and academic areas to meet the specific needs of each student in the group. The school counselor addresses multiple areas of language arts and social skills, while also providing students with remediation in targeted areas of mathematics. The school counselor also reinforces a variety of grade-level appropriate mathematical concepts for all students.

In addition to the benefits to students, standards blending encourages consulting and teaming with teachers. An atmosphere of collaboration with teachers to accomplish student academic achievement goals has the potential to enhance the teacher–school counselor relationship and strengthen universal achievement.

SUMMARY

Implementation of the new vision school counselor's dual roles of educational specialist and mental health specialist and the functions inherent in each role are central to achieving school counseling reform. The school counselor as mental health specialist meets the personal, social, and emotional needs of students within the scope of school counseling. This requires collaboration with professionals within and outside of the school system and the involvement and support of school administrators. The school counselor as educational specialist identifies and removes barriers to academic achievement and, moreover, directly impacts academic achievement through well-planned instructional programming and a working knowledge of academic standards.

The new vision school counselor adeptly combines the roles of educational specialist and mental health specialist using standards blending as an alignment approach that integrates academic and school counseling standards. Standards blending can also be used as a strategy for closing the achievement gap. The school counselor applies differential instructional philosophies with the constructs of Bloom's Taxonomy for creating optimal and individualized curriculum and learning environments.

4

The Predecessor of Accountability: Improving Practices and Demonstrating Effectiveness with Program Evaluation

Program evaluation is an essential competency, legislative mandate, and ethical responsibility of the new vision school counselor. School counselors are obligated by professional accountability to systematically collect and analyze data to determine the usefulness of their educational programs and services in meeting the needs of stakeholders.

Astramovich et al. (2005) define program evaluation as the continuous use of evaluation principles by school counselors to assess and improve the effectiveness of counseling programs and activities. Thus, school counselors gather, examine, and generate data as part of routine, reflective, and investigative practices to facilitate fact-based decision making for optimum functioning.

Program evaluation is a type of action, or applied research that is invaluable in the educational setting where true experiments are extremely difficult due to vast uncontrollable variables and the ethical concerns of randomly assigning children and adolescents to treatment conditions and control groups. As program evaluators, school counselors function as researchers and change agents in a formative mode to determine program impact and to improve systemic programming. Program evaluation is an empowering and powerful proactive strategy for empirical rationale, decision making, change, funding, reform efforts, support, and accountability.

Program evaluation does not equal accountability, but precedes it as a means by which to demonstrate accountable professional practices. Evaluation is a requirement of accountable practices that demonstrates the effectiveness and/or successful implementation of services in measurable terms. Accountability is discussed in greater detail in the next chapter.

In this climate of data-driven and results-based practices, school counselors are required to generate and analyze data, and submit findings to inform the thinking of school administrators and other stakeholders. School administrators use these data to justify resource allocations and the existence of school counseling programs. Other stakeholders use this information to assess the value of school counseling programs in meeting their specific and collective needs.

Just as research-supported practices necessitate that school counselors become savvy consumers of research, demonstrating results-based practices and accountability to stakeholders requires that school counselors become efficient producers of research. It is important that program evaluation become an integral component of the school counseling program's research, review, and feedback structure.

Historically, service logs have been used to document time on task and illustrate the numerous and diverse duties and levels of responsibilities of the school counselor. Service logs often include: community and parent contacts; teacher and colleague consulting; administrative duties; clerical activities; referrals to outside agencies; committee meetings; individual counseling; small group counseling; classroom guidance; professional development activities; staff development and parenting workshops; program coordination; community involvement activities; and lesson planning and curriculum development.

Although services delivered have their value in identifying *what* it is that school counselors do from day to day, they are inadequate in an outcome-driven educational environment. As the axiom goes . . . *we are drowning in information, but starved for knowledge.* Documenting services delivered does not and should not replace program evaluation.

A study by Deck et al. (1990) explored the perceptions of the ASCA leaders pertaining to school counseling research. Program evaluation was identified as the primary critical need area for research in school counseling.

Program evaluation, particularly outcome measures discussed later in this chapter, demonstrate *evidence* over *effort,* and answers the more critical question: how are students different as a result of school counseling programs? Outcome evaluations, however, are in short supply as evidenced in research conducted by Whiston and Sexton (1998) that identified only fifty outcome studies between 1988 and 1995.

Significant concern continues to be expressed regarding the scarcity of school counseling research and program evaluation conducted by counselor educators and supervisors, as well as school counselors. Scarcity of program evaluations that demonstrate and validate school counselor contributions to student development has been the impetus behind the absence of school counselors in education reform agendas and school improvement initiatives.

A spate of research has uncovered a host of reasons for the paucity of practitioner research in school counseling. School counselors indicate a lack of interest, preparation, and comfort level in conducting program evaluations, and a shortage of school counseling–specific program evaluation models and tools (Astramovich et al., 2005). The next chapter provides school counselors with data reporting tools for overcoming these challenges and fully engaging in accountable programming from conception to evaluation.

OUTCOME AND PROCESS EVALUATIONS

The call for program evaluation in school counseling and for collaborative research conducted by practitioners and counselor educators is mounting. Research partnerships benefit both counselor educators and school counseling practitioners. Collaborative studies provide counselor educators with an opportunity to stay apprised of rapidly changing practice needs for teaching and to the reality of the contemporary school setting, and to become involved in applied research in the school setting. Research partnerships with counselor educators provide school counselors with the opportunity to stay abreast of major developments in school counselor preparation, to target professional development activities, and to develop program evaluation skills and comfort levels with data collection, analysis, and reporting. A study conducted by Blackman et al. (2002) highlighted the many benefits of school counselor and counselor educator collaboration, which included renewal, professional development, community, enhanced task completion and creative capacities, and broadened visions.

Program evaluations that measure outcome, that is, the effectiveness of the program in achieving intended goals, are important to establish a causal link between school counseling programs and student change, particularly academic achievement. Outcome evaluations, sometimes referred to as summative evaluations, seek to answer the significant question: *Did it work?*

Program evaluations measure process, that is, program functioning, strengths, weaknesses, and the extent to which the program meets the expectations of and serves the target population. Process evaluations, also known as formative evaluations, are useful for program decision making and program improvement. Process evaluations seek to answer questions such as: *How did it work? How or with what population did it work best?*

School counselors are wise to consider conducting program evaluations that include both measures of process and outcome. Even when outcome measures are positive, additional program data might provide knowledge that can be used to strengthen program outcomes, uncover further needs and unexpected benefits of the program, and identify additional target populations.

PROXIMAL AND DISTAL EVALUATIONS

There has been some debate over the significance of proximal (immediate) vs. distal (long-term) evaluation in linking school counseling program activities to what students know and can do as a result of the program. Brown and Trusty (2005) contend that school counselors need to conduct proximal evaluations in order to establish a causal link between interventions and outcomes vs. distal evaluations that cannot establish such a link due to the number of extraneous variables over time. Distal evaluation outcomes generally do not clearly link school counseling programming to increased achievement due to the great number of factors that impact student achievement. Therefore, school counselors must provide well-defined data that demonstrate enhanced academic achievement that is clearly a result of school counseling programming.

Specific school counseling program activities should be evaluated using proximal evaluation methods such as pre- and post-lesson measures in order to establish correlation, if not causality. Distal evaluations should be conducted as a means of cross validation and support for proximal evaluation outcomes. Proximal data are essential to establishing a distal link. For illustration purposes, consider the following scenario.

The school counselor conducts schoolwide classroom guidance lessons on the topic of study skills, using standards blending, that incorporates both language arts and mathematics curriculum. The school counselor does not include a proximal program evaluation to determine the immediate effects of the lesson on knowledge and skills development. The school counselor and principal, while examining the end-of-year standardized assessment data, note an increase in mathematics and language arts scores for students across grade levels. End-of-year assessment scores are an excellent source of distal data; however, the school counselor cannot confidently claim any credit for the increase in scores because, although the standards-blended lessons clearly demonstrated an overt and direct alignment with the academic curriculum, there are still many other factors that could have contributed to the increase in scores, such as parent involvement, after-school tutoring, remediation programs, and teacher instruction. However, had the school counselor assessed the lesson proximally, that is, immediately before and after implementation, and found a positive impact on knowledge and skills development related to study skills, mathematics, and language arts, the argument could be made and supported.

Over time, consistent program evaluation will aid school counselors in building a strong knowledge foundation from which to expand, enhance, and tailor procedures and programming to the specific needs of a school division. This knowledge structure will allow school counselors and administrators to make declarative statements about the contributions of school counseling and future directions for school counseling programming.

METHODOLOGY

School counseling program evaluation methods can be as diverse as the researcher's imagination. Most methods include behavioral observations, rating scales, student portfolios, and curriculum content instruments. These methods are most often used pre- and postintervention to measure change.

Program evaluations that use *triangulation*, the incorporation of multiple sources of data, strengthen confidence in observed changes. For the same reason, statistical analysis is encouraged using paired sample t-tests for pre- and post-program data in addition to descriptive statistics such as percentages, categories, counts, and frequencies. An analysis of variance (ANOVA) is suggested for analyzing multiple observations,

but attention must be given to statistical assumptions when using an
ANOVA and the MANOVA (Multivariate Analysis of Variance).

The example below illustrates evaluation questions, data sources, and
methods of data analysis of a comprehensive program evaluation conducted by a school counselor in collaboration with counselor educators
(Schellenberg et al., 2007). The evaluation includes both proximal and
distal outcomes, process and outcome measures, multiple observations,
and triangulation.

REDUCING LEVELS OF ELEMENTARY
SCHOOL VIOLENCE WITH PEER MEDIATION

(Schellenberg, Parks-Savage, and Rehfuss, 2007)

EVALUATION QUESTIONS,* DATA SOURCES,
METHODS OF DATA ANALYSIS

Does student knowledge pertaining to conflict, conflict resolution, and
mediation increase as a result of Peace Pal training?
*Data Source: Pre-post-training questionnaire developed from curricu-
lum and administered prior to training, immediately following training,
and three months later.*
Data Analysis: Repeated Measures 1x3 ANOVA
Do peer mediation sessions result in the successful resolution of student
conflict?
Data Source: Peer mediation session records over one academic year.
Data Analysis: Percentages
Do the number of schoolwide out-of-school suspensions decrease with
the implementation of the Peace Pal program?
Data Source: Out-of-school suspension data over a five-year period.
Data Analysis: Frequencies and percentages
Do disputing students who participate in peer mediation sessions view
the sessions as valuable?
Data Source: Peer mediation session records over one academic year.
Data Analysis: Percentages
Do peer mediators perceive the Peace Pal program as valuable?
Data Source: Process questions five years post-program.
Data Analysis: Percentages and qualitative

* Evaluation questions were derived from the goal and objectives of the program.

ETHICAL AND LEGAL CONSIDERATIONS

It is important for school counselors to consider the ethical and legal issues associated with conducting research in the schools. Issues to consider include obtaining parental and student informed consent, confidentiality of assessment data, culture and gender bias in the selection of measures, withholding treatment, and treatment for all students in experimental groups. In addition to a review of the ACA's *Code of Ethics and Standards of Practice* (2005) and the ASCA's *Ethical Standards for School Counselors* (2004), the following resources are beneficial when conducting studies in the public school setting: *Competencies in Assessment and Evaluation for School Counselors* (Association for Assessment in Counseling and Education, 1998); *Counseling and Educational Research* (Houser, 1998); *Guiding Principles for Evaluators* (American Evaluation Association, 1994); *Program Evaluation: Methods and Case Studies* (Posavac and Carey, 2003); *Code of Fair Testing Practices in Education* (Joint Committee on Testing Practices, 2004).

SUMMARY

Program evaluation has been deemed essential by school counseling leadership and educational reform initiatives. It is the school counselor's professional and ethical responsibility to demonstrate, document, and promote accountable practices.

For a variety of reasons school counselors do not engage in program evaluation, despite an increasing demand. Studies have identified the lack of school counselor knowledge and skills in planning and implementing program evaluation as a primary reason.

A lack of applied research has, in turn, created a lack of outcome data for school counseling program support. Practitioner and educator-practitioner research is needed that clearly depicts both the immediate and long-term impact of school counseling prevention and intervention activities on student development, in general, and on student academic achievement in particular.

Debate continues regarding the importance of proximal versus distal evaluations in establishing a causal relationship between school counseling programming and student outcomes. While outcome-based evaluations are in high demand, process evaluations have value as well, suggesting the application of a mixed-method approach. Regardless of the type of evaluation conducted, school counselors need to be aware of the ethical and legal issues associated with conducting research in the school setting.

5

Reporting Accountable Practices

The call for accountability in school counseling practices is not new. A study conducted by Gysbers (2004) of the historical evolution of accountability in school counseling practices dated the call for accountability to the 1920s. The persevering demands for accountability have heightened efforts within the school counseling profession to prepare, encourage, and support school counselor efforts toward accountable practices.

Professional journals are littered with strategies for increasing accountability. Accountability is further emphasized by the initiators of change in school counseling—the CACREP, the ASCA, and the TSCI. Thus, a shift in paradigms requires a shift of the mind not only toward academic- and systems-focused programming, but toward *accountable* academic- and systems-focused programming.

Sustaining the accountability ethic necessitates that school counselors develop needs-driven, standards-based, and research-supported programs, and engage in program evaluation and documentation of outcomes. In order to secure the support of stakeholders and to advance the profession, school counselors must demonstrate how school counseling programs are making a difference in the lives of students, particularly with regard to academic achievement and closing achievement gaps. *To be accountable means being responsible for one's actions and contributions, especially in terms of objectives, procedures, and results. It involves describing goals and what is being done to meet them. It entails collecting information and data that support any accomplishments that can be claimed* (Myrick, 2003, p. 175).

Accountability involves sharing program information and evaluative findings with stakeholders. Studies indicate stakeholder support and partnerships enhance school climate and increase the likelihood of a student's success in school and in life (Bryan, 2005; Cooper, 2002). However, stakeholder support and partnerships are in short supply because, like school administrators, stakeholders in general lack an understanding of the roles and functions of the school counselor and the positive contributions of school counseling programs.

It is vital that school counselors inform stakeholders, primarily school administrators, about the school counselor's dual roles and new vision functions. School counselors who involve stakeholders in program planning and routinely provide stakeholders with information about school counseling activities aid in establishing positive alliances and gaining and maintaining program support.

Information should promote the value of school counseling programs using action plans and results reports. Data reporting should include the components of accountable programming and the impact of school counseling activities on academic achievement and total student development.

Translating data into meaningful reports can be a time-consuming and cumbersome task exacerbated by daunting workloads. Nonetheless, maintaining a comprehensive data reporting system that documents the planning, delivery, and evaluation of data-driven, standards-based, and research-supported services enhances accountability.

Powerful software and computer systems have provided school counselors with the technology to simplify and efficiently manage the process of data collection, analysis, and reporting. And, since necessity is, indeed, the mother of invention, the sections that follow introduce an electronic data reporting system created by a school counselor for school counselors to meet the increasing demands for accountability—a labor of love.

The electronic data reporting system streamlines action planning and results reporting while accommodating the standards blending approach and meeting the programming requirements of the ASCA, TSCI, CACREP, and NCLB.

The system, provided on the enclosed CD-ROM, includes two electronic, user-friendly interactive forms and supporting files for link activation. The system is fully functional using the familiar Microsoft Office 2000 or a more current version.

The *School Counseling Operational Plan for Effectiveness* (SCOPE), illustrated in Figure 5.1, and the *School Counseling Operational Report of Effectiveness* (SCORE), illustrated in Figure 5.2, are accessed using Microsoft Word.

SCOPE

School Counseling Operational Plan for Effectiveness

School: **Counselor:**   **Date:**

Needs Assessment, Data Collection, and Evaluation
Program Type:
☐ Prevention   ☐ Intervention   ☐ Closing-the-Gap Strategy
Evaluation Type:
☐ **Outcome**   ☐ **Process**   ☐ **Proximal**   ☐ **Distal**
Data Source(s):

Details:

Program/Activity Title:

Goal(s)-Objective(s)

Target Population
Students in Grade(s):   Other:

Details:

Method of Delivery
☐ Small Group   ☐ Classroom Guidance
☐ Presentation/Workshop   ☐ Other

Research-Supported Program Curriculum
Number of lessons/sessions:
Program/Lesson Activities and Timeline:

National Standards Addressed
Mathematics
☐ Number and Operations
☐ Algebra
☐ Geometry
☐ Measurement
☐ Data Analysis & Probability
☐ Problem Solving
☐ Reasoning and Proof   *(continued)*

☐ Communication
☐ Connections
☐ Representation

Language Arts

☐ Listen and Speak
☐ Read
☐ Write

School Counseling

☐ Academic
☐ Personal/Social
☐ Career

State Standards/Additional Information

Figure 5.1.

SCOPE and SCORE have embedded macros in order to increase the power and functionality of the data reporting system. If your macro security is set on high, macros are automatically disabled and you will experience limited form functionality while using SCOPE and SCORE. If your macro security is set on medium, you will be prompted to choose whether or not you wish to enable macros when you open SCOPE and SCORE, in which case the user should select *enable macros* because you know that the macros in the data reporting system are legitimate. If your macro security is set at low, which is the setting often used by those who have virus protection on their computers, you will not be prompted and you will have full functionality while using SCOPE and SCORE.

To change macro security using Word 2000, select Tools, Macro, Security (adjust the level of security for functionality as noted above), and click OK. To change macro security using Word 2002/2003 XP, select

SCORE

School Counseling Operational Plan for Effectiveness

School: **Counselor:**   **Date:**

Activity Title

Goal(s)-Objective(s)

Data Collection and Evaluation

Number of Program Participants: Grade(s):   Other:

Evaluation Type:

☐ **Outcome**   ☐ **Process**   ☐ **Proximal**   ☐ **Distal**

Data Source(s):

Details:

Method(s) of Data Analysis

☐ Percentages   ☐ Means/Averages   ☐ Frequencies

☐ Counts   ☐ Statistical Testing   ☐ Other

Details:

Evaluation Outcome/Program Impact

The program was Select One in meeting program goal(s) and targeted objective(s) in the following area(s):

☐ Academic   ☐ Personal/Social   ☐ Career

☐ Closing the Achievement Gap

Details:

Directions for Future Programming

☐ Continue Implementation of Current Activity

☐ Modify Activity Based on Results

Details:

Figure 5.2.

Tools, Options, Security, Macro Security (adjust the level of security for functionality as noted above), and click OK.

SCOPE and SCORE and the six supporting files on the CD are read-only access so that the user cannot inadvertently delete the School Counseling Data Reporting System (SCDRS) folder or files contained within the folder. The easiest way to copy the data reporting system files is to use Microsoft Explorer and simply drag the entire SCDRS folder into a folder on your hard drive. The user can also apply the "save as" function to accomplish the task. SCOPE and SCORE are then fully accessible on the hard drive, and can be saved to diskettes and CDs, printed, and e-mailed. Store the read-only SCOPE and SCORE CD in a safe place for use again in the event of hard drive failure or inadvertent deletion from your hard drive.

Each time SCOPE and SCORE are opened the user should apply the "save as" function to preserve clear forms for subsequent uses. Otherwise, with each subsequent use the user will need to clear each field, type over, or save the read-only CD-ROM files to the hard drive again.

The tab key and mouse should be used when navigating SCOPE and SCORE. If the return key is used and space is inadvertently added into the form, just delete the space—you cannot delete the formatting or fields, so relax! Only the SCORE worksheet and graph can be deleted in order to accommodate user preferences. The worksheet and graph can be easily reinserted if deleted inadvertently, or if the user should decide to include the worksheet and/or graphic illustration at a later date. SCOPE and SCORE were created for school counselors by a school counselor, who understands the importance of *user-friendly*!

The following are abbreviated instructions and navigation tips for getting started with SCOPE and SCORE using Microsoft Office 2000 or more recent version.

Insert CD-ROM and save all files to your hard drive.
The SCDRS folder files will include:

SCOPE
SCORE
Support_Graph SCORE
Support_Worksheet SCORE
Support_Possible Data Sources
Support_School Counseling Standards

Support_Mathematics Standards
Support_Language Arts Standards

Remove the CD.

Open SCOPE (action plan) or SCORE (results report). SCOPE and SCORE contain embedded macros for increased power and functionality. Macro security must be set on low in order to obtain full functionality in SCOPE and SCORE. Macro security and how to adjust macro settings are discussed above.

Although support files can be opened and reviewed, there is no need to directly open support files when completing SCOPE and SCORE because the files are embedded in the forms and available upon clicking italicized links, graphic illustration, and worksheet icon within the forms:

SCOPE

Data Sources (links to possible data sources)
Mathematics (links to national mathematics standards)
Language Arts (links to national language arts standards)
School Counseling (links to national school counseling standards)

SCORE

Data Sources (links to possible data sources)
Graph illustration (double click to complete—may delete or reinsert if inadvertently deleted)
Worksheet icon (double click to input/analyze data—may delete or reinsert if inadvertently deleted)

Once SCOPE and SCORE are opened use the "save as" function with a name that is representative of the program/activity being documented. Otherwise, clear the form or retrieve it from the CD.

Simply use your mouse or tab key to navigate the forms.

Fill in the blanks and check boxes that apply.

SCOPE and SCORE meet the essential component guidelines for action planning, closing the achievement gap action planning, and results reporting recommended by the ASCA (2005). Although intended to be used together to demonstrate essential components of a comprehensive school counseling program that aligns with academic achievement missions, SCOPE and SCORE can be used separately for action planning and results reporting, respectively. SCOPE and SCORE are most powerful, however, when united to comprise a system of accountability that demonstrates credible, comprehensive programming, an overt alignment with academic achievement missions, and the direct impact of school counseling programs on total student development from conception to evaluation. Data from SCOPE and SCORE can be used for professional publication and presentation, for data-driven program improvement and decision making, and for communicating with stakeholders and eliciting stakeholder support for new vision school counseling programs.

ACTION PLANNING WITH SCOPE

Abraham Lincoln declared "give me six hours to chop down a tree and I will spend the first four sharpening the axe." Lincoln's statement clearly depicts the time-consuming and important nature of planning. SCOPE reduces planning time for school counselors and ensures the inclusion of essential components needed for the creation and submission of comprehensive and succinct action plans.

The ASCA (2005) recommends that school counselors create both curriculum action plans and closing the gap action plans. SCOPE accommodates both types of action plans in one efficient form. In addition, SCOPE is not limited to classroom lessons and closing the achievement gap. SCOPE is designed to create action plans for all programs and activities specific to school counseling.

SCOPE makes use of form check boxes and text boxes to walk the user through the process of accountable program planning. SCOPE includes links for quick and easy access to an exhaustive list of data sources for needs assessment and measuring program impact.

SCOPE eliminates the need for school counselors to refer to several different sources for identifying academic and school counseling standards while creating action reports. SCOPE includes links that provide the user with fast access to complete lists of the following national standards: the ASCA school counseling standards, the NCTM mathematics standards, and the NCTE language arts standards.

When completing SCOPE, users must identify program need and how need was established; chapter 2 is useful for completing this section.

When identifying objectives, keep in mind that objectives are specific, measurable, and linked directly to program need. Also, keep in mind that a program or activity may be data-driven and standards-based, provide prevention and intervention, and serve as a strategy for closing the achievement gap when completing the section entitled Needs Assessment, Data Collection, and Evaluation.

SCOPE is designed to assist in identifying data sources during the program planning process for needs assessment and program evaluation. Double clicking on the italicized *Data Sources* text in the Needs Assessment, Data Collection, and Evaluation section links the user to the list of possible data sources. The user may decide upon multiple data sources to include in the *SCOPE* Data Sources text box. Click the X in the upper right hand corner of your screen to return to SCOPE from the possible data sources list.

In many cases the data source for program evaluation is the same as that used for needs identification. For example, if student attendance records revealed low attendance rates and, thus, an objective of the program or activity included increasing student attendance, then student attendance records should be reviewed again at a specified post-program date. In some cases, however, the data source used for needs assessment will differ from that used for program evaluation. Figure 5.3 illustrates a standards-blended conflict resolution program for second grade students, which was created in response to a needs assessment and evaluated using a pre- and post-program instrument. Note that the school counselor provided clarification in the Details text box of the Needs Assessment, Data Collection, and Evaluation section.

When identifying target population(s), the text box entitled Details allows for more specific identifications that may include gender, ethnicity, economic status, special needs, and so on. For example, the Target Population section might read Students in Grade 8 and the Details text box would further delineate that the students are African American males from a low socioeconomic background.

SCOPE accommodates the planning and implementation of the standards-blending approach discussed in chapter 3, which includes the national mathematics and language arts standards and the school counseling standards. Simply double click on the italicized *Mathematics*, *Language Arts*, and *School Counseling* text in the National Standards Addressed section to link to a comprehensive list of each set of national standards. These standards are printed in the appendices of this text as well.

Users can simply check the broad applicable standards in SCOPE or list each specific standard–student competency identified in the SCOPE text boxes for more detailed reporting as illustrated in Figure 5.3. SCOPE also provides a section entitled State Standards/Additional Information for users, who elect to include state academic and school counseling standards and other information deemed useful.

SCOPE

School Counseling Operational Plan for Effectiveness

School: Virginia Public Schools

Counselor: Schellenberg   **Date:** 3/31/07

Needs Assessment, Data Collection, and Evaluation

Program Type:
☑ Prevention   ☑ Intervention   ☐ Closing-the-Gap Strategy

Evaluation Type:
☑ Outcome   ☐ Process   ☑ Proximal   ☐ Distal

Data Source(s): Pre-post lesson assessment

Details: Second grade teachers and students indicated a need for conflict resolution strategies. Data collected for program evaluation using an assessment instrument from curriculum content to measure objects 1 and 3.

Program/Activity Title:

Resolving Conflict Peacefully and Enhancing Academic Achievement in Mathematics and Language Arts

Goal(s)-Objective(s)

To enhance students' personal/social, career, and academic development.

Objective 1: Students will define conflict, understand the nature of the conflict, and be introduced to a positive approach to problem-solving for improving interpersonal relations.

Objective 2: Students will learn a 4-step problem-solving method.

Objective 3: Students will gain a better understanding of sets and fractional representations.

Target Population

Students in Grade(s):   2   Other:
Details: Classroom guidance activities were selected based on grade level need.

Method of Delivery

☐ Small Group   ☑ Classroom Guidance   ☐ Presentation/Workshop
☐ Other

Research-Supported Program Curriculum

Number of lessons/sessions: 5

Program/Lesson Activities and Timeline:

Five lessons to five classes will be completed in 10 school days from the date of this report. The lessons is 40 minutes.
Icebreaker: School counselor writes FNOLITC on the board for students to unscramble as CONFLICT.
Discussion: Definition and nature of conflict are presented. Approaches to resolving conflict are discussed. The 4-step problem-solving method is introduced as such an approach. Students are encouraged to share and participate.
Activities: The 4 steps on large magnetized strips are placed on the board. Students read and role play multiple conflict scenarios to demonstrate each step. The process is then presented as a set of four items and fractional representations.

National Standards Addressed

Mathematics

☑ Number and Operations NUM PK-2.1–2.3
☑ Algebra ALG.PK-2.1–2.4
☐ Geometry
☐ Measurement
☑ Data Analysis & Probability DATA.PK-2.1, 2.2
☑ Problem Solving PROB.PK-12.1–12.4
☐ Reasoning and Proof
☑ Communication PROB.COMM.PK-12.1–12.4

(continued)

☑ Connections PROB.CONN.PK-12.1–12.3
☑ Representation PROB.REP.12.1–12.3

Language Arts

☑ Listen and Speak NLA.4, NLA.7, NLA.9, NLA
☑ Read NLA.2, NLA.3
☐ Write

School Counseling

☑ Academic A1.1-5, A2.3–4, A3.1–3,5, B1.2
☑ Personal/Social A1.5, A1.8, A2.608, B1.1, B1.6
☑ Career A2.1, C2.2

State Standards/Additional Information

Virginia Math 2.4, Eng 2.1-2.3;
Virginia Language Arts: EA8; EC4; EC5; EP2; EP4
Virginia School Counseling:

Academic: EA8
Career: EC4, EC5
Personal/Social: EP2, EP4

Figure 5.3.

DATA ANALYSIS AND RESULTS
REPORTING WITH SCORE

Documentation and presentation of program outcomes should be translated into brief, understandable, and meaningful results. As noted earlier in this text, data analysis and reporting have been identified by school counselors as difficult aspects of program evaluation. SCORE is designed to simplify the process of program evaluation for school counselors including ease of data analysis, graphic illustration, and results reporting.

SCORE accommodates all types of program evaluation as well as short-term, intermediate, or long-term program evaluation schedules as recommended by the ASCA. SCORE is designed to walk the user through the process of accountable program evaluation using form check boxes, text boxes, and drop-down menus. Like SCOPE, SCORE can be as brief or as detailed as the user desires.

Although SCORE can be used apart from SCOPE, keep in mind that SCORE includes only a brief description of the program, primarily focusing on the program's outcome and future programming direction. It is SCOPE that provides stakeholders with the detailed description and essential components of the program and the core academic and school counseling standards addressed in the program.

When completing the section entitled Goal(s)-Objectives, keep in mind that this section should mirror that of SCOPE when used together. As noted earlier, the optimal power of the school counseling data reporting system is in the combined use of SCOPE and SCORE for a more comprehensive system of accountability.

Like SCOPE, SCORE links to possible data sources for evaluating program impact. Double clicking on the italicized *Data Sources* text in the section entitled Data Collection and Evaluation links the user to a comprehensive list of possible data sources for evaluating program effectiveness. Click the X in the upper right hand corner of your screen to return to SCOPE from the Data Sources list.

Best practices dictate that the method of data collection for program evaluation be determined during program planning. For this reason, the method of data collection for program evaluation should mirror that listed in SCOPE. The data source(s) used for needs assessment may differ, or not, as discussed earlier in this chapter.

You know what they say about the best-laid plans. Therefore, should the method of data collection for program evaluation listed in SCORE differ from that of SCOPE when used together, this deviation from the plan should be explained in the Details text box of the Data Collection and Evaluation section of SCORE.

The SCORE worksheet accommodates one of the most widely used methods of proximal evaluation in education, which is the quantitative pre- and post-program measure. Once the collection of pre- and post-lesson data is complete and ready to be analyzed, double click on the icon at the bottom of SCORE labeled Pre-Post Data Worksheet. This icon will link the user to a preformulated Excel Worksheet (see Figure 5.4). Worksheet cells containing formulas have been protected to avoid inadvertent deletion.

Pre- and Post-Program Data Worksheet

Program Title:

Data Type:

Pre-Program Data	Post-Program Data	Pre-Program Data Mean	Post-Program Data Mean	Percentage of Change Pre- to Post-Program
		50	100	100%
50	100			

Figure 5.4.

The worksheet can be used to calculate means and percentages of difference for up to five thousand data sets. Pre- and post-program data are typed into columns A and B. The pre-program mean score appears in column C; the post-program mean score appears in column D. The percentage of difference from pre- to post-program measure appears in column E.

The SCORE worksheet can be used to analyze data for an entire school's population, individual students, a single class, multiple classes, grade levels, special populations, and specific question clusters for determining change/growth in targeted areas such as school counseling curriculum components, language arts components, and mathematics components. The worksheet can be copied for the inclusion of multiple worksheets in order to disaggregate data, or the worksheet can be deleted for exclusion from the report. If multiple worksheets are desired, either cut and paste the worksheet or insert another, using Insert, Objects on the Word tool bar, identifying the file Support_SCORE Worksheet for insertion.

Should the user elect not to include access to the worksheet and raw data in SCORE, which may be the case depending upon the target audience, the support file entitled Support_SCORE Worksheet can be accessed and used to store and analyze data. Once the file is opened the user would use the "save as" function to rename the worksheet file, or multiple worksheets in one file with the copy and paste feature, to reflect the associated program and data.

SCORE allows the user to enhance results reporting with graphic representations—remember, a picture is worth a thousand words! To complete the graph, double click on it and modify the content to reflect the data. Like the worksheet, the graph can be deleted or duplicated for multiple graphic representations. If multiple graphs are desired, either cut and paste the graph or insert another using Insert, Objects on the Word tool bar, identifying the file Support_SCORE Graph for insertion.

Also like the worksheet, if the user would like to have graphic representation but does not wish to include it in SCORE, the support file entitled Support_SCORE Graph can be accessed. Once opened the user would use the "save as" function to rename the graph, or multiple graphs in one file with the copy and paste feature, to reflect the associated program and data.

Figure 5.5 illustrates the use of a pre- and post-program method of evaluation and the application of data desegregation using multiple worksheets and multiple graph representations for more detailed reporting.

SCORE

School Counseling Operational Report of Effectiveness

School: Virginia Public Schools

Counselor: Schellenberg **Date:** 3/31/07

Activity Title
Resolving Conflict Peacefully and Enhancing Academic Achievement in Mathematics and Language Arts

Goal(s)-Objective(s)
To enhance students' personal/social, career, and academic development.

Objective 1: Students will define conflict, understand the nature of conflict, and be introduced to a positive approach to problem-solving for improving interpersonal relations.
Objective 2: Students will learn a 4-step problem-solving method.
Objective 3: Students will gain a better understanding of sets and fractional representations.

Data Collection and Evaluation
Number of Program Participants: 103   Grade(s): 2   Other:

Type of Evaluation:
☑ Outcome   ☐ Process   ☑ Proximal   ☐ Distal
Data Source(s): Pre-Post Lesson Assessment

(continued)

Details: Classroom guidance activities were selected by grade level need. Assessment instrument developed from curriculum content to measure success in meeting objects 1 and 3.

Method(s) of Data Analysis

☑ Percentages   ☑ Means/Averages   ☐ Frequencies
☑ Counts   ☑ Statistical Testing ☐ Other

Details: Student knowledge on the target topics was assessment immediately prior to the lesson and following the lesson using the same instrument.

Evaluation Outcome/Program Impact

The program was effective in meeting program goal(s) and targeted objective(s) in the following area(s):

☑ Academic   ☑ Personal/Social   ☐ Career
☐ Closing the Achievement Gap

Details: The standards-blending lesson was effective in meeting both target objects 1 and 3. Knowledge development occurred on both the school counseling and academic curriculum contents for students in all classrooms and for both subgroups, which was statistically significant as determined by paired sample t-tests. Independent sample t-tests indicated no significant differences between minority and non-minority proficiency levels on the core academic curriculum content. This would indicate the absence of an achievement gap between the two subgroups at pre-and post-lessons. Refer to the attached graphs.

Directions for Future Programming

☑ Continue Implementation of Current Activity
☐ Modify Activity Based on Results

Details: This program illustrates the significant impact of standards-blending for teaching school counseling curriculum and reinforcing academic curriculum. Although, students had already been taught the mathematical concepts presented, there was a significant increase in proficiency as a result of the standards-blending lesson.

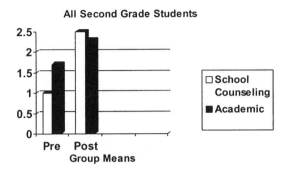

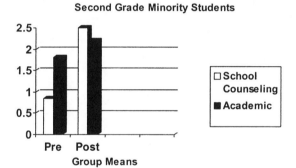

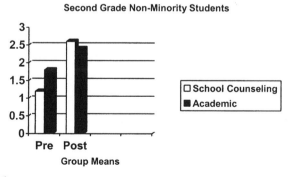

Figure 5.5.

Using information technologies, the SCOPE and SCORE can be shared quickly and conveniently with stakeholders via electronic mail, Web sites, file transfers, and multimedia presentations. The electronic nature of the SCOPE and SCORE and the vast information infrastructure of the Internet allow school counselors to efficiently share data reports anytime from anywhere.

SUMMARY

Accountability in education and school counseling practices is a growing trend. Accountable practices necessitates that school counselors create action plans and results reports that identify data-driven, standards-based, and research-supported services, and specify program goals, procedures, and evaluative outcomes.

Reports should include, at a minimum, the essential components identified in the ASCA national model. SCOPE and SCORE, an electronic data reporting system specific to school counseling, include the essential components identified by the ASCA and support the use of standards blending. Together, SCOPE and SCORE provide school counselors with a proficient means for creating comprehensive operational plans and results reports.

6

Implications for School Counselor Preparation and Practice

Reform-minded leadership that extends beyond the school counseling profession to all stakeholders, namely school administrators, is key to the successful implementation of a new paradigm and to the ultimate transformation of school counseling. Building an accountable school counseling profession that directly aligns with the academic achievement missions of schools requires a collective effort, motivation, and a positive attitude toward change.

During this time of unprecedented transition and growth toward more academic- and systems-focused practices, it is important that the school counselor's professional identity continue to reflect the role of mental health specialist. Although school counselors focus on academic achievement, it is with the caveat that student safety and well-being are first and foremost—there can be no casualties in our quest for higher academic achievement. As such, school counselors must be well-prepared to handle the same significant and challenging issues encountered by any professional counselor.

On a regular basis, school counselors make decisions regarding a litany of problems inherent in a turbulent society that include the following: suspected child abuse, alcohol and drug use, suicide ideation, homicide ideation, child custody disputes, child and teen pregnancy, family dysfunction, and sexual activities of minors. School counselors must know the law and have the clinical competence vital to appropriate responding in their role as mental health specialist.

Appropriate responding may mean the difference between life and death and litigation or not. As long as counseling remains a function of the school counselor, then providing the highest quality mental health services to children and adolescents is the legal and ethical responsibility of school counseling practitioners. School administrators, charged with the selection of highly qualified school counselors and school counselor supervisors and directors, consequently determine the caliber of their school counseling teams.

The level of clinical competence of a school counselor is evidenced by advanced education and credentialing. Advanced level credentialing by the National Board of Certified Counselors (NBCC) should be encouraged to enhance the clinical competence of school counselors. Advanced level credentialing by the National Board for Professional Teaching Standards (NBPTS) should be encouraged to enhance the instructional competence of school counselors by a teacher-governed credentialing board. One must not be pitted against the other, but unfortunately this is the case at present.

As noted in chapter 1, one advanced school counseling credential that combines both clinical and instructional competencies and is governed by both NBCC and NBPTS is ideal. Such a credential would reflect both the educational specialist and mental health specialist roles of the new school counselor. Providing equal support and incentives for acquiring either or both the NBCC and the NBPTS advanced credentials for school counselors serves to strengthen the professional identity of the new school counselor and may induce renegotiations between the two boards.

Strengthening the professional identity of school counselors as educators and mental health providers requires consistency in the use of the language that defines a renewed school counseling profession. Language determines the way in which important others within and outside of school counseling perceive the profession.

Altering the language of the profession has proven to be a difficult task even for the most conscientious reform-minded stakeholders, due to the enduring nature of the historical language stronghold rooted in the guidance movement. Nonetheless, stakeholders are encouraged to intensify efforts to purge outdated vernacular from contemporary school counseling.

Stakeholders are encouraged to replace *guidance counselor* with *school counselor* and the *guidance office* with the *counseling office*. The ASCA recommends that *professional school counselor* be used to replace *guidance counselor*. Whether using *school counselor* or *professional school counselor*, diligence is needed to permeate the system.

Change that improves a part of the system, toward the goal of the system, improves the whole system. So, as we endeavor collectively to strengthen a valuable and endangered part of the educational system, we are developing the system as a whole.

COUNSELOR EDUCATOR

The transformation of school counseling begins with counselor educators, who create and shape the attitude, knowledge, skills, and abilities that school counselors bring to the practice setting. Counselor educators use a variety of educational and instructional philosophies, models, and techniques so as to provide pre-service school counselors with a broad repertoire of approaches and tools vital to practice in a setting that is changing at dizzying rates.

This text provides counselor educators with pragmatic tools and approaches for preparing new vision school counselors to be proactive in anticipating academic- and systems-focused programming and accountable practices. When introducing pre-service school counselors to the information and resources in this text, it is important to stress that the ultimate goal is to practice accountable programming on a daily basis — not once in a while. Like administrators, counselor educators understand that accountability in school counseling, and education and counseling in general, is not new, and it is here to stay.

Meeting the challenges of contemporary school counseling necessitates that counselor educators teach to the new vision for school counseling. Teaching from an academic- and systems-focused pedagogy that illustrates the practical needs of schools, current trends and developments in school counseling and education, school reform initiatives, and school administrator expectations, prepares pre-service school counselors for the realities of practice.

Unquestionably, preparing the quintessential new vision school counselor is no small task.

Pedagogy

Due to historical adoption of the mental health-focused pedagogy for school counseling, counselor educators are well-experienced and adept

in providing clinical instruction that stresses the application of counseling theory and counseling techniques, particularly as it applies to minors, as well as the legal and ethical considerations of counseling practices in the school setting. Counselor educator expertise in this area is
indispensable to clinical competency and must continue in order for the
new vision school counselor to practice skillfully in the role of mental
health specialist for children and adolescents.

It is important, however, for counselor educators to ensure that pre-
service school counselors understand the scope of school counseling
practices, specifically with regard to providing mental health–related
services to students. Ensuring that pre-service school counselors can
distinguish between appropriate and inappropriate services, and understand situations in which collaboration and referral within and outside
of the school are necessary, is vital to the safety of children. Additionally, understanding the scope of clinical counseling in a school setting
is analogous to the optimal delivery of mental health–related services.

Counselor educators, who introduce the national and state academic
content standards in addition to the school counseling standards, are
preparing pre-service school counselors for the role of educational specialist and the expectations of school administrators. Requiring pre-
service school counselors to apply both sets of standards, differential instruction, and Bloom's constructs in the planning and delivery of lessons provides opportunities to practice and build necessary skills in
these areas. Having pre-service school counselors apply these strategies
using diverse student populations, group topics, and group sizes reflects
the realities of professional practice in a culturally pluralistic educational system.

Teaching standards blending as a fixed and integral appendage to
comprehensive school counseling models such as the ASCA national
model, provides pre-service school counselors with a solid foundation
and framework from which to build an integrative, academic-focused
program that school administrators can readily support. Standards
blending is also an excellent approach for fulfilling CACREP founda-
tions and contextual dimensions for school counseling program standards and the knowledge and skills requirements for school counselors.

The new paradigm heightens the educational specialist role of the
school counselor, which can be polished by pre-service school counselor involvement in education and training related to instruction. En-

couraging (or requiring) pre-service school counselor participation in instructional foundation courses emphasizes and develops an attitude toward academic-focused practices. Counselor educators can guide pre-service school counselors toward the selection of appropriate courses as part of their electives or supplemental training outside of school. Also, involving pre-service school counselors in collaborative research projects with school counseling practitioners provides an applied means by which to develop instructional and teaching skills.

Counselor educators might also incorporate curriculum development, instructional strategies, and classroom management, as well as student assessment, achievement, and learning styles into school counseling courses and experiential learning. Strengthening pre-service school counselor knowledge and skills in these instructional-related areas can aid in abolishing teaching requirements for school counselor licensure, discussed in chapter 3, which continues in a few states.

Bridging New Vision Theory and Practice

Bridging theory and practice requires an understanding of theory and practice. Counselor educators might begin by reviewing current school reform legislation and trends in education. Perusing research and literature that describes the shortcomings of school counseling and how the profession is viewed by stakeholders, namely school administrators, is an excellent way to introduce the Transforming School Counseling Initiative (TSCI).

For example, counselor educators might want to share studies such as the one conducted by Zalaquett (2005), which describes what school administrators consider to be high priority for school counseling programs. Group dialogue and literature reviews pertaining to the issues that prompted a new vision for school counseling are essential to a thorough understanding of the needs of contemporary practice.

Discussions about the importance of, and how to secure, school administrator support with regard to implementing the new paradigm assists pre-service school counselors in understanding current and future challenges and in developing dialogue for partnership building. Doses of reality early in the program aid in establishing an understanding of professional practice in a dynamic climate defined by accelerated change.

For example, having school administrators from both the elementary and secondary levels serve as guest lecturers or engage in candid round-table discussions in the classroom aids pre-service school counselors in understanding the immediate needs of schools and role expectations of administrators. Engaging in experiential learning activities enhances knowledge of school environments, norms, policies, and procedures and increases the likelihood of successful academic-focused programming in practice.

As pre-service school counselors begin to develop an understanding of the relationship between new vision theory and practice, practical approaches and tools are necessary to guide the implementation of accountable academic- and systems-focused programming. Teaching students to use alignment approaches such as standards blending and data reporting tools such as SCOPE and SCORE meets CACREP standards, the recommendations of the ASCA and the TSCI, and school improvement initiatives, all of which emphasize technology, accountability, and universal academic achievement.

CACREP underscores the importance of preparing pre-service school counselors to meet the realities of contemporary practice that include increased diversity and advanced technology. The student-centered, integrative nature of standards blending coupled with differential instructional practices and Bloom's constructs is ideal for developing pre-service school counselor knowledge and skills related to meeting the diverse needs of students and developing strategies for closing the achievement gap.

Having pre-service school counselors document standards blending in program planning, delivery, and evaluation using SCOPE and SCORE introduces them to school counseling–specific technology. In addition to exemplifying the application of technology in school counseling practices, SCOPE and SCORE are invaluable teaching and learning tools that walk pre-service school counselors through new vision school counseling programming from planning to evaluation.

Early and continuous practical experiences in school counseling settings maximize opportunities for applying standards blending and bridging new vision school counseling theory and practice, while informing traditional school counseling practices. New vision school counselor interns who introduce standards blending, SCOPE, and SCORE to traditional-minded practitioners during internships promote accountability and the academic-focused paradigm. New vision interns have the potential to permeate settings where the mental health-focused paradigm continues to prevail and data reporting systems are absent or inadequate. These pre-service school counselors, armed with new vision tools and approaches, can effect change in practice.

Research Collaboration

Collaborative research partnerships between counselor educators and school counseling practitioners are powerful alliances with the potential to improve educational and professional school counseling practices and student academic achievement. Reform-minded counselor educators take advantage of every opportunity to actively engage in collaborative research that adds to the body of literature and supports academic- and systems-focused school counseling programs.

Research collaboration with practitioners also addresses the immediate need to train currently practicing school counselors in data collection, data analysis, results interpretation, and program evaluation methodology. School counselors who learn these essential skills through the research collaboration process are in a better position to continue engaging in evaluative studies that support the efficacy of new vision programming. In turn, school counselors can provide counselor educators with access to the practice and research setting and an understanding of the unique needs of the school/division.

Collaborating on the publication of research outcomes aids in developing practitioner skills in scholarly publication, while also promoting the positive impact and value of new vision school counseling services on academic achievement and total student development. Publication informs and benefits all stakeholders, demonstrating how theory drives practice and how practice, in turn, informs theory.

SCHOOL COUNSELOR

Changing the pedagogy in counselor education to reflect the new academic- and systems-focused paradigm is fundamental to achieving school counseling reform. However, unless these changes occur in practice the new vision remains theory, and school counselors risk losing their jobs. A professional survival mentality may be warranted, as some districts have already eliminated school counselor positions due to role confusion, role conflict, and role inconsistency in addition to a lack of data supporting the school counselor's value as a partner in academic achievement. The need to establish the profession as one that squarely contributes to student academic achievement and gains the leadership and support of school administrators is gaining momentum.

Much work is ahead that requires a commitment to change. School counselors must take the road less traveled and partner with school administrators, apply approaches that directly and overtly align with academic development, create action plans and results reports, and share programming practices and outcomes. School counselors are urged to make use of technology as a vehicle to fortify accountability and professional advocacy efforts.

Changing to a new paradigm and engaging in unfamiliar practices creates internal struggle for many individuals. Stay positive and focused—struggle strengthens us and creates growth. Somewhere in the struggle emerges a higher level of excellence, enthusiasm, and passion for the profession.

It is an exciting time to be a part of the school counseling profession as we strive to establish the school counselor as an indispensable member of the educational team. United in our efforts, practical application of the new vision is imminent.

New Vision Programming

Accepting the challenge to implement systemic change and raise the academic achievement of all students with collaborative accountable programming requires: (a) gaining leadership and support of school administrators, (b) establishing advisory committees, (c) assuming the roles of mental health specialist and educational specialist, (d) collecting and examining data for needs-driven programming, (e) blending of academic and school counseling standards, (f) developing research-supported curriculum, (g) conducting program evaluations, (h) using available technology, and (i) creating and disseminating action plans and results reports. School counselors can rise to the challenge using this text as a guide.

Using the standards-blending approach, school counselors are no longer implying an alignment with academic achievement missions but demonstrating the alignment in an overt and direct manner. School counselors who become accustomed to routinely applying standards blending as a permanent appendage to the comprehensive school counseling program are implementing new vision practices and promoting lasting change in school counseling.

Keep in mind that standards blending can be extended beyond the classroom. School counselors can team with parents to identify a broad range of issues and topics of importance to parents and families (e.g., safety at home and in the community, chores, deployment, familial relationships). School counselors can hold small group workshops that teach parents how to blend their child's academic standards into personal/social topics discussed at home. Parents who engage in standards blending with their students are imparting important life skills while reinforcing academics in targeted areas.

Standards blending to a school counselor is like a blank canvas to an artist. Working with school administrators, parents, students, teachers, and data, the possibilities for effecting change, heightening academic achievement, closing the achievement gap, and enhancing total student development are limited only by the boundaries of the school counselor's creative mind. Do not hesitate to seek out ideas and feedback from stakeholders—harness the creative power of collective minds!

Documentation of standards-blended programs and outcomes are not benefiting anyone if the information stays in the closet. Action plans and results reports must be shared. School counselors who want to ensure accountable programming and the creation of reports that include the components deemed essential by the ASCA and school administrators are encouraged to use SCOPE and SCORE. SCOPE and SCORE navigate school counselors through what are, for many, foreign waters. SCOPE and SCORE can be disseminated in seconds to efficiently communicate information to stakeholders, namely school administrators, that demonstrates *how* the new school counselor is making a difference in the lives of children—one program at a time.

Transitioning with Technology

Technology broadens the school counselor's potential for professional advocacy. Over a billion people use the Internet for professional and personal reasons, making this information infrastructure a powerful and pervasive communication tool.

The Internet provides school counselors with a broad-reaching, practical, and proficient medium for communication with stakeholders. Mass communication is particularly important during this time of transitioning to a new paradigm. School counselors need to inform stakeholders about the changing landscape of school counseling and how these changes improve services and strengthen the profession.

Van Horn and Myrick (2001) emphasize the importance of school counselors becoming literate in information technology in order to meet the demands of the information age. Van Horn and Myrick identified technology, particularly the Internet, as an important mechanism in determining the success of school counseling programs, yet many school counselors do not have a presence on the Web. Those school counselors with a presence on the Web are not generally using the site to inform stakeholders, reverse historical trends, and promote the emerging new vision paradigm and a renewed profession.

For example, a recent review of 456 school counselor Web sites conducted by Milsom and Bryant (2006) revealed a lack of information pertaining to professional advocacy. Departmental Web sites did not include the beliefs and practices of new vision school counselors, information regarding current trends and developments such as the TSCI, new vision programming, or the adoption of the term *school counselor* to replace *guidance counselor*. The outcome of Milsom and Bryant's investigation leaves one to believe that school counselors and administrators are unaware or nonsupportive of the new paradigm and the transformation of school counseling, or that they are resistant to change.

School counselors can use Web sites to provide information for the support of systems that facilitate the mission of new vision school counseling programs. Web sites can also be used to shape perceptions and effect change in systems that have not adopted the new paradigm.

New vision school counseling programs become that much more meaningful and credible when stakeholders have an understanding of practices and programming and view the school counselor as a knowledgeable professional. Therefore, at the very least Web sites should communicate (a) school counselor roles and functions, (b) school counselor education, training, and credentials, (c) information regarding professional associations, (d) current trends and developments in the profession to include the ASCA model and TSCI, and (e) mission statements and program goals that clearly connect school counseling to the academic achievement mission.

School counselors are encouraged to explore the plethora of computer technology applications. In addition to professional advocacy, advanced technology can be used by school counselors for the following: clinical supervision, group and individual consultation, conferencing, online mentoring and peer mediation, database sharing, research and professional development, information retrieval and dissemination, career development, prevention and intervention activities, and assistive devices and services for special-needs and diverse populations.

Professional Identity and Advocacy

Promoting a unified professional identity and engaging in professional advocacy necessitates that school counselors stay abreast of the research and current trends and developments that impact new vision school counseling practices. Remaining proficient in the profession involves reading professional journals and newsletters, maintaining professional association memberships, attending conferences, and networking with counseling professionals within and outside of the school setting to include counselor educators. School counselors use this information to enhance practices and to promote unified roles, functions, and the language of the profession.

Lifelong learning is essential in this young profession that is experiencing unprecedented change and rapid growth. Continuous professional development allows school counselors to astutely communicate with stakeholders and to effectively meet the needs of students with the continuous improvement of new vision practices.

Clearly articulating the school counselor's new vision roles and functions to stakeholders, primarily school administrators is important, however; let us not forget the familiar cliché, *actions speak louder than words*. Thus, consistently demonstrating how school counseling programs contribute to academic achievement and total student development is the most effective means of professional advocacy and establishing a professional identity for school counselors.

Teaming with other educators in the planning and delivery of services is another valuable means by which to advocate for the renewed profession that views collaboration as an endless resource. The new school counselor actively seeks out opportunities to work with colleagues, teachers, counselor educators, administrators, and parents. Collective efforts generally enhance programming. Additionally, working with stakeholders helps the school counselor to stay visible and active in meeting the academic, personal/social, and career development needs of all students.

Standards blending provides an ideal opportunity for collaboration with classroom teachers, who genuinely appreciate the reinforcement of academic standards within and outside of the classroom. School counselors can team with resource teachers, such as art and music teachers, to provide creative and dramatic musicals and assemblies that involve students, include academic and school counseling standards, and can be presented to the entire student body. This is also a great way to get parents and the community involved in programming. The sky is the limit when standards blending is used as a springboard from which to launch comprehensive programming.

School counselors can also make a difference outside of the school building, which will positively affect practices inside of the school building and promote the transformation of school counseling. School counselors might consider attending and presenting at professional education and counseling conferences and in the community, joining or establishing a regional school counseling leadership team, joining professional associations, serving as an officer on professional associations or credentialing boards, and engaging in research collaboration with counselor educators.

School counselors might also consider presenting on new vision school counseling topics at staff development meetings to an audience of school administrators. School administrators appreciate insight into the changes that are occurring in the school counseling profession. School administrators also value fresh ideas as to how those changes can enhance student achievement and contribute to school improvement.

School counselors know *how* school counseling makes a difference in the lives of children, but we have been negligent in demonstrating an overt alignment with, and direct impact on, academic achievement. We have also been lax in providing stakeholders with essential documentation that depicts accountable practices and positive program outcomes, which establishes the value of our profession. It is time to get off the sidelines and into the game—the clock is running and many are keeping score!

SCHOOL COUNSELOR SUPERVISOR

School counselor supervisors are in a unique position to represent the interests of both school administrators and school counselors. The traditional paradigm was somewhat problematic for the school counselor supervisor, who had some difficulty defining how the school counselor's roles and functions clearly contributed to academic achievement and aligned with the school's mission. The implied nature of contributions to student development, primarily academic achievement, has not been enough to fully secure support for school counseling programs.

The compatible interests and aligned missions of school administrators and new vision school counselors provides enthusiastic school counselor supervisors with a new platform from which to promote change. Many school administrators and school counseling practitioners are still unaware of the full scope of the current movement to transform the profession of school counseling, making advocacy for the new vision a priority and groundbreaking experience for reform-minded school counselor supervisors.

In addition to professional advocacy and promoting a unified professional identity, reform-minded school counselor supervisors are charged with the task of gaining support for, and implementing, school counselor roles and new vision functions. School counselor supervisors encourage and provide professional development opportunities to school counselors, particularly information and training that pertains to the practice of new vision school counseling. School counselor supervisors also aid in the selection of highly qualified reform-minded school counselors.

Implementing School Counselor Roles and New Vision Functions

Reform-minded school counselor supervisors create school counselor job descriptions and performance evaluations to reflect the new vision school counselor's roles and functions at the elementary and secondary levels. School counselor supervisors and administrators can refer to the CACREP standards, ASCA national model, TSCI, state standards for school counseling programs, and this text for guidance in redefining school counselor duties and responsibilities under the new paradigm.

Job descriptions and performance expectations identify the essential functions of new vision school counselors at each educational level. This is particularly important for pertinent school counselor performance evaluation and for identifying job-related search criteria for school counselor recruitment and selection.

Selecting New Vision School Counselors

Principals do not generally have a background or education in school counseling and may be unaware of the current paradigm shift, yet are often responsible for hiring school counselors. Therefore, it is imperative that school counselor supervisors provide guidance to school administrators in selecting reform-minded school counselors.

The level of guidance provided by the school counselor supervisor is largely dependent upon the size of the school and school district. Guidance may entail working closely with principals to provide selection criteria and standardized interview questions. Guidance might also require the supervisor's direct participation in the screening of applications and interviewing of prospective school counselor candidates.

Professional Development

This text provides school counselor supervisors with the information, approaches, and tools for fulfilling their administrative supervision role under the new paradigm. However, fulfillment of the clinical supervision role requires graduate-level training in counseling and counselor supervision in addition to advanced state and national counselor credentialing.

School counselor supervisors are urged to continue their education and professional development specific to counselor supervision, namely models of supervision specific to counseling. Understanding and developing the ability to apply models of counselor supervision is vital to the optimal functioning of the individual school counselor as well as the school counseling team.

In addition to education and progressive credentials, school counselor supervisors add to their credibility as an advanced level school counselor and effective leader by remaining actively involved in the profession. School counselor supervisors are expected to maintain professional association membership, present at conferences, publish in peer-reviewed journals, and collaborate with counselor educators.

When school counselors view the counselor supervisor as credible, they are more likely to be open to leadership and to actively seek out the supervisor for opportunities to develop higher-level knowledge and skills. In addition to credibility, the school counselor supervisor must be viewed as approachable, nonconfrontational, and nonjudgmental. An atmosphere that welcomes questions, views mistakes as an opportunity for growth, and demonstrates a team approach to obtaining answers and specialized knowledge is conducive to learning and optimal functioning. School counselors will seek answers from colleagues, which may or may not be correct in the absence of an approachable school counselor supervisor.

It is important for school counselor supervisors to accept that they cannot and will not know it all. While an approachable attitude and advanced education and counselor credentials are essential to optimal administrative and clinical competence, as well as effective leadership, having all the answers is not. Our ever changing, global workforce is exceedingly specialized. An effective leader is a resourceful visionary who consults with those most knowledgeable in a particular area and/or program and engages in a needs-driven, team approach to decision making, process and program implementation, and systemic change.

Changing traditional ways of responding to student needs is particularly challenging for even the most adept school counselors. The reform-minded supervisor is a lifeline for school counselors who are not knowledgeable of the Transforming School Counseling Initiative and who are having difficulty implementing the new paradigm.

School counselor supervisors model desired new vision practices and provide professional development opportunities to school counselors for understanding and fulfilling their dual roles and functions. School counselor supervisors provide school counselors with administrative and clinical supervision, and information, tools, and approaches for implementing accountable, comprehensive school counseling programs that align with district and state academic achievement missions. Therefore, it is recommended that supervisors conduct professional development workshops that teach and apply the standards-blending method and demonstrate the use of SCOPE and SCORE as tools for documenting the ASCA-recommended action plans and results reports.

Encouraging the use of standards blending as an affixed appendage to the comprehensive school counseling program clearly positions the program under the umbrella of the new paradigm and academic achievement mission of schools. Including SCOPE and SCORE as tools to be used by school counselors for developing accountable programs and documenting impact data provides counselor supervisors with advocacy instruments to share with school administrators.

School administrators look to school counselor supervisors for program data that support the department's services and progress toward school improvement and universal academic achievement. The electronic nature of SCOPE and SCORE allow operational plans and results reports to be stored for access by all school counselors within a division for shared programming and optimal data-driven student services.

Providing formal professional development sessions using the National School Counselor Training Initiative (NSCTI) MetLife modules aids in educating school counselors on new vision practices. Each of the four modules takes approximately one hour to present and demonstrates a variety of activities that contribute to educational equity, closing the achievement gap, assessment, and the use of data.

As newly acquired knowledge and skills are applied and the school counseling program begins to transform, so, too, does the individual school counselor, which may create unanticipated conflict and discomfort for some. It is important for school counseling supervisors to understand that in the midst of change even the most seasoned school counselors may experience many of the same thoughts and feelings of uncertainty and dependency of a beginning school counselor. School counselor supervisors, anticipating the struggle, foresee the stumbling, which they meet with encouragement, problem solving, and a focus on what is being learned while on the road to discovery.

Understanding developmental models of counselor supervision is extremely useful, particularly during this time of paradigmatic change. It may be necessary to temporarily adjust levels of counselor supervision until the challenged school counselor regains perceptions of competence and stability.

Meeting challenges with a positive attitude and a focus on the shared new vision for school counseling reduces resistance while individuals and the system seek to reestablish homeostasis. Eventually, homeostasis is restored, and the outcome is worth the journey.

SCHOOL ADMINISTRATOR

It has been a decade since implementation of the Transforming School Counseling Initiative. Still, there is a dearth of commentary in the field on this major development, with many school divisions continuing to go about business as usual. Several factors are contributing to this reluctance or inability to cede the traditional school counseling paradigm.

Some within the profession fear that the new paradigm threatens the status quo, and so remain shackled to traditional mental health- and individual-focused practices. Others simply prefer the comfort of complacency over change. Still others are unaware of the movement to transform school counseling or lack a practical process, approach, and tools for implementing a different paradigm.

School administrators have not been fully informed, or have been misinformed, regarding the paradigmatic change underway and movement to transform school counseling. And, since the successful implementation of the new paradigm is inextricably tied to school administrator acceptance and stewardship, this text is designed to: (a) serve as the communication conduit for understanding new vision school counseling and the dual roles and functions of the new school counselor, (b) provide the impetus for the development of a symbiotic relationship between school administrators and school counselors, (c) promote change in school counseling programming and practices toward accountable practices and an academic- and systems-focused model, and (d) emphasize the importance of school counselor and school counselor supervisor selection and promotion practices in ensuring highly qualified, reform-minded school counseling teams driven by a shared vision.

School administrator leadership is the essential missing link to institutionalizing new vision school counseling and fully transforming school counseling—a laudable child-first goal. School administrators who support the dual roles of the new vision school counselor hire highly qualified reform-minded school counselors and supervisors and require the implementation of alignment approaches and the documentation of program plans and outcomes; they are ushering in a new era for school counseling and school systems.

Supporting the New Vision and a Unified Professional Identity

Over the years, school counselors have been assigned duties and responsibilities that are unrelated to school counseling due to inconsistent pedagogies in counselor education, role ambiguity, and a lack of accountability in professional practices. For example, many school counselors are maintaining student records, supervising study halls, serving as meeting secretaries, acting as substitute teachers and/or disciplinarians, operating attendance tables, and assisting the front office clerical staff. Studies show that assignment to noncounseling duties are taking up to 50 percent of school counselors' time (Burnham and Jackson, 2000) and are not cost-efficient or an effective use of manpower (Hardesty and Dillard, 1994).

Instead, school counselors could be identifying low-achieving populations and developing programs designed to have a direct positive impact on closing achievement gaps. School counselors could also be enhancing students' motivation to learn, attend school, and graduate through systemic interventions, collaboration with teachers, and the implementation of standards blending.

Together, reform-minded school administrators and school counselor supervisors, principals, and school counselors can develop a unified plan that directs the implementation of the dual roles of the school counselor and ensuing functions at both the elementary and secondary levels. Guiding appropriate performance toward the new school counselor's roles and functions is essential to the ultimate elimination of arbitrary and inappropriate duties that are hindering efforts to implement academic- and systems-focused programs.

On the threshold of this exciting migration to a new vision for school counseling, school administrators can expect to encounter resistance. Resistance is a hurdle to overcome and one that is not new to school administrators. School counselors and school counselor supervisors with an allegiance to the traditional paradigm are likely to challenge reform-minded administrators to a paradigm debate. Such a challenge is lamentable, but not unanticipated and met with analytic simplicity—the TSCI's new vision for school counseling is recognized in the profession as an essential, pragmatic, and theoretically sound movement that is in the best interest of all stakeholders.

Selecting New Vision School Counselor Supervisors

School administrators are vicariously responsible for the actions and inactions of school counseling practitioners. As such, it is in the best interest of school administrators to look beyond the minimal competencies of master's degrees and mandatory licensure by states' departments of education when selecting school counselors and school counselor supervisors and directors. As more school administrators base selection and promotion decisions on a preference for school counselors who hold advanced-level credentialing more school counseling practitioners will seek to obtain such credentials.

Hiring highly qualified school counselor supervisors (and school counselors) who have discarded the traditional school counseling model in favor of the new paradigm is essential to implementation of academic- and systems-focused programs. The ASCA offers information regarding the purpose, duties, responsibilities, and required and desired qualifications of a school counselor supervisor on their Web site at www.schoolcounselor.org.

The need for at least one highly qualified school counselor supervisor in each school division has been well-documented. What has not been so well-documented is the need to hire reform-minded school counselor supervisors who are knowledgeable of, and in agreement with, the TSCI and understand the roles and functions of the new school counselor.

School counselor supervisors should have a track record of presentation and publication demonstrative of self-initiated professional development and a deeper knowledge and understanding of contemporary school counseling practices. Highly qualified school counselor supervisors have the education, training, and credentials to provide both clinical and administrative supervision.

Preparation for the clinical and administrative supervision of school counselors includes education beyond the master's level, school counseling experience and endorsement at the elementary and secondary levels, and training in counselor supervision and models of counselor supervision. Additionally, school counselor supervisors hold the credentials of National Certified Counselor (NCC) and National Certified School Counselor (NCSC), indicative of optimal preparation as a counselor and school counselor. Advanced voluntary credentials also demonstrate a commitment to professional development and a motivation toward professional advancement and skills improvement. Ideally, school counselor supervisors possess a doctoral degree in counselor supervision and state licensure as a professional counselor.

Having administrative and clinical expertise are essential to school counselor leadership and to directing the school counselor's dual roles of educational specialist and mental health specialist. School counselors who have access to clinical supervision experience enhanced counseling skills, effectiveness, and accountability; increased confidence and competence; and are more motivated toward professional development (Agnew et al., 2000; Crutchfield and Borders, 1997). Clinical supervision also assists school counselors in enhancing their counseling and decision-making skills for more effective management of routinely complex cases and for ensuring optimal student development and a safe school environment.

Responding adequately to student needs that may involve severe depression, homicide and suicide ideation, substance abuse, school violence, child abuse, and pregnancy requires that school counseling practitioners apply proficient clinical skills and knowledge of the legal and ethical implications of their actions or inactions. For these reasons, school counselors have expressed their desire and need for meaningful administrative and clinical supervision in order to remain competent. Studies have found, however, that most school counselors are not receiving clinical supervision of any kind due to a lack of highly qualified school counselor supervisors (Kaffenberger et al., 2006; Page et al., 2001).

Limited qualified applicant pools have resulted in the promotion of practicing school counselors as a result of their performance as school counselors, or the promotion of individuals with higher education or supervisory experience in areas other than school counseling. Alas, proficiency as a school counselor or an administrator trained in other educational fields does not equal a proficient school counselor supervisor.

Although such practices may have been necessary, research has revealed that school counselor supervisors who lack specialized education in counselor supervision tend to shy away from the clinical aspects of enhancing counseling knowledge and skills, thereby providing insufficient clinical supervision (Herlihy et al., 2002). Insufficient clinical supervision, which includes the ethical and legal implications of counseling minors in the schools, leaves many school districts chronically vulnerable to litigation.

School counselors and others who aspire to provide administrative and clinical counselor supervision should seek to acquire advanced education and credentialing in preparation for such a role. *Putting in one's time* as a school counselor simply is not sufficient to earn one's *rite of passage* to promotion.

School counselors who have a passion for the profession, a desire to effect change, and an aspiration to become highly competent, effective leaders will seek to enhance education and credentials above the minimal criteria for school counselor and contribute to the profession through research, presentation, and publication. These are the school counselors who have prepared for the clinical and administrative roles of counselor supervisor, earning their rite of passage to promotion.

As noted earlier, school administrators can encourage advanced-level education and credentialing for school counselors by demonstrating this preference in promotion and selection decisions. In addition to motivation toward professional development, offering pay supplements and/or higher salaries to the new school counselor in directorship and supervisory positions is a financial investment that will prove to have substantial returns for all stakeholders.

SUMMARY

Decades of political winds have shifted the educational climate, shaping our nation's schools. School counselors are continuously left out of educational reform agendas, viewed as noncontributors, and burdened with large student caseloads because we cannot provide evidence of academic-focused programming and our positive impact on academic achievement—the primary mission of schools. Concern for the future of the profession and recognizing the need to align school counseling programs with academic achievement for optimal student services has prompted the need for an unparalleled reform movement in school counseling.

School counseling reform requires fundamental shifts in both preparation and practice. It is an exciting and challenging time to be a part of the school counseling profession, with much work to be done and significant changes to be made—together.

Appendix A

National Mathematics Standards

(National Council of Teachers of Mathematics, NCTM, 2000)

PREKINDERGARTEN—SECOND

Number and Operations

NM-NUM.PK-2.1

Understand numbers, ways of representing numbers, relationships among numbers and number systems.

1. Count with understanding and recognize how many in sets of objects.
2. Use multiple models to develop initial understandings of place value and the base-ten number system.
3. Develop understanding of the relative position and magnitude of whole numbers and of ordinal and cardinal numbers and their connections.
4. Develop a sense of whole numbers and represent and use them in flexible ways, including relating, composing, and decomposing numbers.
5. Connect number words and numerals to the quantities they represent, using various physical models and representations.
6. Understand and represent commonly used fractions, such as 1/4, 1/3, and 1/2.

NM-NUM.PK-2.2

Understand meanings of operations and how they relate to one another.

1. Understand various meanings of addition and subtraction of whole numbers and the relationship between the two operations.
2. Understand the effects of adding and subtracting whole numbers.
3. Understand situations that entail multiplication and division, such as equal groupings of objects and sharing equally.

NM-NUM.PK-2.3

Compute fluently and make reasonable estimates.

1. Develop and use strategies for whole-number computations, with a focus on addition and subtraction.
2. Develop fluency with basic number combinations for addition and subtraction.
3. Use a variety of methods and tools to compute, including objects, mental computation, estimation, paper and pencil, and calculators.

Algebra

NM-ALG.PK-2.1

Understand patterns, relations, and functions.

1. Sort, classify, and order objects by size, number, and other properties.
2. Recognize, describe, and extend patterns such as sequences of sounds and shapes or simple numeric patterns and translate from one representation to another.
3. Analyze how both repeating and growing patterns are generated.

NM-ALG.PK-2.2

Represent and analyze mathematical situations and structures using algebraic symbols.

1. Illustrate general principles and properties of operations, such as commutativity, using specific numbers.
2. Use concrete, pictorial, and verbal representations to develop an understanding of invented and conventional symbolic notations.

NM-ALG.PK-2.3

Use mathematical models to represent and understand quantitative relationships.

1. Model situations that involve the addition and subtraction of whole numbers using objects, pictures, and symbols.

NM-ALG.PK-2.4

Analyze change in various contexts.

1. Describe qualitative change, such as student's growing taller.
2. Describe quantitative change, such as student's growing two inches in one year.

Geometry

NM-GEO.PK-2.1

Analyze characteristics and properties of two- and three-dimensional geometric shapes and develop mathematical arguments about geometric relationships.

1. Recognize, name, build, draw, compare, and sort two- and three-dimensional shapes.
2. Describe attributes and parts of two- and three-dimensional shapes.
3. Investigate and predict the results of putting together and taking apart two- and three-dimensional shapes.

NM-GEO.PK-2.2

Specify locations and describe spatial relationships using coordinate geometry and other representational systems.

1. Describe, name, and interpret relative positions in space and apply ideas about relative position.
2. Describe, name, and interpret direction and distance in navigating space and apply ideas about direction and distance.

3. Find and name locations with simple relationships such as "near to" and in coordinate systems such as maps.

NM-GEO.PK-2.3

Apply transformations and use symmetry to analyze mathematical situations.

1. Recognize and apply slides, flips, and turns.
2. Recognize and create shapes that have symmetry.

NM-GEO.PK-2.4

Use visualization, spatial reasoning, and geometric modeling to solve problems.

1. Create mental images of geometric shapes using spatial memory and spatial visualization.
2. Recognize and represent shapes from different perspectives.
3. Relate ideas in geometry to ideas in number and measurement.
4. Recognize geometric shapes and structures in the environment and specify their location.

Measurement

NM-MEA.PK-2.1

Understand measurable attributes of objects and the units, systems, and processes of measurement.

1. Recognize the attributes of length, volume, weight, area, and time.
2. Compare and order objects according to these attributes.
3. Understand how to measure using nonstandard and standard units.
4. Select an appropriate unit and tool for the attribute being measured.

NM-MEA.PK-2.2

Apply appropriate techniques, tools, and formulas to determine measurements.

1. Measure with multiple copies of units of the same size, such as paper clips laid end to end.
2. Use repetition of a single unit to measure something larger than the unit, for instance, measuring the length of a room with a single meter stick.
3. Use tools to measure.
4. Develop common referents for measures to make comparisons and estimates.

Data Analysis & Probability

NM-DATA.PK-2.1

Formulate questions that can be addressed with data; collect, organize, and display relevant data to answer.

1. Pose questions and gather data about themselves and their surroundings.
2. Sort and classify objects according to their attributes and organize data about the objects.
3. Represent data using concrete objects, pictures, and graphs.

NM-DATA.PK-2.2

Select and use appropriate statistical methods to analyze data.

1. Describe parts of the data and set of data as a whole to determine what the data show.

NM-DATA.PK-2.3

Develop and evaluate inferences and predictions that are based on data.

1. Discuss events related to students' experiences as likely or unlikely.

Problem Solving

NM-PROB.PK-12.1

Build new mathematical knowledge through problem solving.

NM-PROB.PK-12.2

Solve problems that arise in mathematics and in other contexts.

NM-PROB.PK-12.3

Apply and adapt a variety of appropriate strategies to solve problems.

NM-PROB.PK-12.4

Monitor and reflect on the process of mathematical problem solving.

Reasoning & Proof

NM-PROB.REA.PK-12.1

Recognize reasoning and proof as fundamental aspects of mathematics.

NM-PROB.REA.PK-12.2

Make and investigate mathematical conjectures.

NM-PROB.REA.PK-12.3

Develop and evaluate mathematical arguments and proofs.

NM-PROB.REA.PK-12.4

Select and use various types of reasoning and methods of proof.

Communication

NM-PROB.COMM.PK-12.1

Organize and consolidate their mathematical thinking through communication.

NM-PROB.COMM.PK-12.2

Communicate their mathematical thinking coherently and clearly to peers, teachers, and others.

NM-PROB.COMM.PK-12.3

Analyze and evaluate the mathematical thinking and strategies of others.

NM-PROB.COMM.PK-12.4

Use the language of mathematics to express mathematical ideas precisely.

Connections

NM-PROB.CONN.PK-12.1

Recognize and use connections among mathematical ideas.

NM-PROB.CONN.PK-12.2

Understand how mathematical ideas interconnect and build on one another to produce a coherent whole.

NM-PROB.CONN.PK-12.3

Recognize and apply mathematics in context and outside of mathematics.

Representation

NM-PROB.REP.PK-12.1

Create and use representations to organize, record, and communicate mathematical ideas.

NM-PROB.REP.PK-12.2

Select, apply, and translate among mathematical representations to solve problems.

NM-PROB.REP.PK-12.3

Use representations to model and interpret physical, social, and mathematical phenomena.

GRADES THREE–FIVE

Number and Operations

NM-NUM.3-5.1

Understand numbers, ways of representing numbers, relationships among numbers and number systems.

1. Understand the place-value structure of the base-ten number system and be able to represent and compare whole numbers and decimals.
2. Recognize equivalent representations for the same number and generate them by decomposing and composing numbers.
3. Develop understanding of fractions as parts of unit wholes, as parts of a collection, as locations on the number lines, and as divisions of whole numbers.
4. Use models, benchmarks, and equivalent forms to judge the size of fractions.
5. Recognize and generate equivalent forms of commonly used fractions, decimals, and percents.
6. Explore numbers less than 0 by extending the number line and through familiar applications.
7. Describe classes of numbers according to characteristics such as the nature of their factors.

NM-NUM.3-5.2

Understand meanings of operations and how they relate to one another.

1. Understand various meanings of multiplication and division.
2. Understand the effects of multiplying and dividing whole numbers.
3. Identify and use relationships between operations, such as division as the inverse of multiplication to solve problems.
4. Understand and use properties of operations, such as the distributivity of multiplication over addition.

NM-NUM.3-5.3

Compute fluently and make reasonable estimates.

1. Develop fluency with basic number combinations for multiplication and division and use these combinations to mentally compute related problems such as 30 × 50.
2. Develop fluency in adding, subtracting, multiplying, and dividing whole numbers.
3. Develop and use strategies to estimate the result of whole-number computations and to judge the reasonableness of such results.
4. Develop and use strategies to estimate computations involving fractions and decimals in situations relevant to students' experiences.
5. Use visual models, benchmarks, and equivalent forms to add and subtract commonly used fractions and decimals.
6. Select appropriate methods and tools for computing with whole numbers from among mental computations, estimation, calculators, and paper and pencil according to the contest and nature of the computation and use the selected method or tools.

Algebra

NM-ALG.3-5.1

Understand patterns, relations, and functions.

1. Describe, extend, and make generalizations about geometric and numeric patterns.
2. Represent and analyze patterns and functions, using words, tables, and graphs.

NM-ALG.3-5.2

Represent and analyze mathematical situations and structures using algebraic symbols.

1. Identify such properties as commutativity, associativity, and distributivity and use them to compute with whole numbers.
2. Represent the idea of a variable as an unknown quantity using a letter or a symbol.
3. Express mathematical relationships using equations.

NM-ALG.3-5.3

Use mathematical models to represent and understand quantitative relationships.

1. Model problem situations with objects and use representations such as graphs, tables, and equations to draw conclusions.

NM-ALG.3-5.4

Analyze change in various contexts.

1. Investigate how a change in one variable relates to a change in a second variable.
2. Identify and describe situations with constant or varying rates of change and compare them.

Geometry

NM-GEO.3-5.1

Analyze characteristics and properties of two- and three-dimensional geometric shapes and develop mathematical arguments about geometric relationships.

1. Identify, compare, and analyze attributes of two- and three-dimensional shapes and develop vocabulary to describe the attributes.
2. Classify two- and three-dimensional shapes according to their properties and develop definitions of classes of shapes such as triangles and pyramids.
3. Investigate, describe, and reason about the results of subdividing, combining, and transforming shapes.
4. Explore congruence and similarity.
5. Make and test conjectures about geometric properties and relationships and develop logical arguments to justify conclusions.

NM-GEO.3-5.2

Specify locations and describe spatial relationships using coordinate geometry and other representational systems.

1. Describe location and movement using common language and geometric vocabulary.
2. Make and use coordinate systems to specify locations and to describe paths.
3. Find the distance between points along horizontal and vertical lines of a coordinate system.

NM-GEO.3-5.3

Apply transformations and use symmetry to analyze mathematical situations.

1. Predict and describe the results of sliding, flipping, and turning two-dimensional shapes.
2. Describe a motion or a series of motions that will show that two shapes are congruent.
3. Identify and describe line and rotational symmetry in two- and three-dimensional shapes and designs.

NM-GEO.3-5.4

Use visualization, spatial reasoning, and geometric modeling to solve problems.

1. Build and draw geometric objects.
2. Create and describe mental images of objects, patterns, and paths.
3. Identify and build a three-dimensional object from two-dimensional representations of that object.
4. Identify and draw a two-dimensional representation of a three-dimensional object.
5. Use geometric models to solve problems in other areas of mathematics, such as number and measurement.

6. Recognize geometric ideas and relationships and apply them to other disciplines and to problems that arise in the classroom or in everyday life.

Measurement

NM-MEA.3-5.1

Understand measurable attributes of objects and the units, systems, and processes of measurement.

1. Understand such attributes as length, area, weight, volume, and size of angle and select the appropriate type of unit for measuring each attribute.
2. Understand the need for measuring with standard units and become familiar with standard units in the customary and metric systems.
3. Carry out simple unit conversions such as from centimeters to meters, within a system of measurement.
4. Understand that measurements are approximations and how differences in units affect precision.
5. Explore what happens to measurements of a two-dimensional shape such as its perimeter and areas when the shape is changed in some way.

NM-MEA.3-5.2

Apply appropriate techniques, tools, and formulas to determine measurements.

1. Develop strategies for estimating the perimeters, areas, and volumes of irregular shapes.
2. Select and apply appropriate standard units and tools to measure length, area, volume, weight, time, temperature, and the size of angles.
3. Select and use benchmarks to estimate measurements.
4. Develop, understand, and use formulas to find the area of rectangles and related triangles and parallelograms.

5. Develop strategies to determine the surface areas and volumes of rectangular solids.

Data Analysis & Probability

NM-DATA.3-5.1

Formulate questions that can be addressed with data; collect, organize, and display relevant data to answer.

1. Design investigations to address questions and consider how data-collection methods affect the nature of the data set.
2. Collect data using observations, surveys, and experiments.
3. Represent data using tables and graphs such as line plots, bar graphs, and line graphs.
4. Recognize the differences in representing categorical and numerical data.

NM-DATA.3-5.2

Select and use appropriate statistical methods to analyze data.

1. Describe the shape and important features of a set of data and compare related data sets, with an emphasis on how the data are distributed.
2. Use measures of center, focusing on the median, and understand what each does and does not indicate about the data set.
3. Compare different representations of the same data and evaluate how well each representation shows important aspects of the data.

NM-DATA.3-5.3

Develop and evaluate inferences and predictions that are based on data.

1. Propose and justify conclusions and predictions that are based on data and design studies to further investigate the conclusions or predictions.

NM-DATA.3-5.4

Understand and apply basic concepts of probability.

1. Describe events as likely or unlikely and discuss the degree of likelihood using such words as certain, equally likely, and impossible.
2. Predict the probability of outcomes of simple experiments and test the predictions.
3. Understand that the measure of the likelihood of an event can be represented by a number from 0 to 1.

Problem Solving

NM-PROB.PK-12.1

Build new mathematical knowledge through problem solving.

NM-PROB.PK-12.2

Solve problems that arise in mathematics and in other contexts.

NM-PROB.PK-12.3

Apply and adapt a variety of appropriate strategies to solve problems.

NM-PROB.PK-12.4

Monitor and reflect on the process of mathematical problems solving.

Reasoning & Proof

NM-PROB.REA.PK-12.1

Recognize reasoning and proof as fundamental aspects of mathematics.

NM-PROB.REA.PK-12.2

Make and investigate mathematical conjectures.

NM-PROB.REA.PK-12.3

Develop and evaluate mathematical arguments and proofs.

NM-PROB.REA.PK-12.4

Select and use various types of reasoning and methods of proof.

Communication

NM-PROB.COMM.PK-12.1

Organize and consolidate their mathematical thinking through communication.

NM-PROB.COMM.PK-12.2

Communicate their mathematical thinking coherently and clearly to peers, teachers, and others.

NM-PROB.COMM.PK-12.3

Analyze and evaluate the mathematical thinking and strategies of others.

NM-PROB.COMM.PK-12.4

Use the language of mathematics to express mathematical ideas precisely.

Connections

NM-PROB.CONN.PK-12.1

Recognize and use connections among mathematical ideas.

NM-PROB.CONN.PK-12.2

Understand how mathematical ideas interconnect and build on one another to produce a coherent whole.

NM-PROB.CONN.PK-12.3

Recognize and apply mathematics in context and outside of mathematics.

Representation

NM-PROB.REP.PK-12.1

Create and use representations to organize, record, and communicate mathematical ideas.

NM-PROB.REP.PK-12.2

Select, apply, and translate among mathematical representations to solve problems.

NM-PROB.REP.PK-12.3

Use representations to model and interpret physical, social, and mathematical phenomena.

GRADES SIX–EIGHT

Number and Operations

NM-NUM.6-8.1

Understand numbers, ways of representing numbers, relationships among numbers and number systems.

1. Work flexibly with fractions, decimals, and percents to solve problems.
2. Compare and order fractions, decimals, and percents efficiently and find their approximate locations on a number line.
3. Develop meaning for percents greater than 100 and less than 1.
4. Understand and use ratios and proportions to represent quantitative relationships.

5. Develop an understanding of large numbers and recognize and appropriately use exponential, scientific, and calculator notations.
6. Use factors, multiples, prime factorization, and relative prime numbers to solve problems.
7. Develop meaning for integers and represent and compare quantities with them.

NM-NUM.6-8.2

Understand meanings of operations and how they relate to one another.

1. Understand the meaning and effects of arithmetic operations with fractions, decimals, and integers.
2. Use the associative and commutative properties of addition and multiplication and the distributive property of multiplication over addition to simplify computations with integers, fractions, and decimals.
3. Understand and use the inverse relationships of addition and subtraction, multiplication and division, and squaring and finding square roots to simplify computations and solve problems.

NM-NUM.6-8.3

Compute fluently and make reasonable estimates.

1. Select appropriate methods and tools for computing with fractions and decimals from among mental computation, estimation, calculators or computers, and paper and pencil, depending on the situation, and apply the selected methods.
2. Develop and analyze algorithms for computing with fractions, decimals, and integers and develop fluency in their use.
3. Develop and use strategies to estimate the results of rational-number computations and judge the reasonableness of the results.
4. Develop, analyze, and explain methods for solving problems involving proportions such as scaling and finding equivalent ratios.

Algebra

NM-ALG.6-8.1

Understand patterns, relations, and functions.

1. Represent, analyze, and generalize a variety of patterns with tables, graphs, words, and when possible symbolic rules.
2. Relate and compare different forms of representations for a relationship.
3. Identify functions as linear or nonlinear and contrast their properties from tables, graphs, or equations.

NM-ALG.6-8.2

Represent and analyze mathematical situations and structures using algebraic symbols.

1. Develop an initial conceptual understanding of different uses of variables.
2. Explore relationships between symbolic expressions and graphs of lines, paying particular attention to the meaning of intercept and slope.
3. Use symbolic algebra to represent situations and to solve problems, especially those that involve linear relationships.
4. Recognize and generate equivalent forms for simple algebraic expressions and solve linear equations.

NM-ALG.6-8.3

Use mathematical models to represent and understand quantitative relationships.

1. Model and solve contextualized problems using various representations, such as graphs, tables, and equations.

NM-ALG.6-8.4

Analyze change in various contexts.

1. Use graphs to analyze the nature of changes in quantities in linear relationships.

Geometry

NM-GEO.6-8.1

Analyze characteristics and properties of two- and three-dimensional geometric shapes and develop mathematical arguments about geometric relationships.

1. Precisely describe, classify, and understand relationships among types of two- and three-dimensional objects using their defining properties.
2. Understand relationships among the angles, side lengths, perimeters, areas, and volumes of similar objects.
3. Create and critique inductive and deductive arguments concerning geometric ideas and relationship such as congruence, similarity, and the Pythagorean relationship.

NM-GEO.6-8.2

Specify locations and describe spatial relationships using coordinate geometry and other representational systems.

1. Use coordinate geometry to represent and examine the properties of geometric shapes.
2. Use coordinate geometry to examine special geometric shapes, such as regular polygons or those with pairs of parallel or perpendicular sides.

NM-GEO.6-8.3

Apply transformations and use symmetry to analyze mathematical situations.

1. Describe sizes, positions, and orientations of shapes under informal transformations such as flips, turns, slides, and scaling.

2. Examine the congruence, similarity, and line or rotational symmetry of objects using transformations.

NM-GEO.6-8.4

Use visualization, spatial reasoning, and geometric modeling to solve problems.

1. Draw geometric objects with specified properties such as side lengths or angle measures.
2. Use two-dimensional representations of three-dimensional objects to visualize and solve problems such as those involving surface area and volume.
3. Use visual tools such as networks to represent and solve problems.
4. Use geometric models to represent and explain numerical and algebraic relationships.
5. Recognize and apply geometric ideas and relationships in areas outside the mathematics classroom, such as art, science, and everyday life.

Measurement

NM-MEA.6-8.1

Understand measurable attributes of objects and the units, systems, and processes of measurement.

1. Understand both metric and customary systems of measurement.
2. Understand relationship among units and convert from one unit to another within the same system.
3. Understand, select, and use units of appropriate size and type to measure angles, perimeter, area, surface area, and volume.

NM-MEA.6-8.2

Apply appropriate techniques, tools, and formulas to determine measurements.

1. Use common benchmarks to select appropriate methods for estimating measurements.

2. Select and apply techniques and tools to accurately find length, area, volume, and angle measurements to appropriate levels of precision.
3. Develop and use formulas to determine the circumference of circles and the area of triangles, parallelograms, trapezoids, and circles and develop strategies to find the area of more complex shapes.
4. Develop strategies to determine the surface area and volume of selected prisms, pyramids, and cylinders.
5. Solve problems involving scale factors, using the ratio and proportion.
6. Solve simple problems involving rates and derived measurements for such attributes as velocity and density.

Data Analysis & Probability

NM-DATA.6-8.1

Formulate questions that can be addressed with data; collect, organize, and display relevant data to answer.

1. Formulate questions, design studies, and collect data about a characteristic shared by two populations and different characteristics within one population.
2. Select, create, and use appropriate graphical representations of data, including histograms, box plots, and scatter plots.

NM-DATA.6-8.2

Select and use appropriate statistical methods to analyze data.

1. Find, use, and interpret measures of center and spread, including mean and interquartile range.
2. Discuss and understand the correspondence between data sets and their graphical representations, especially histograms, stem-and-leaf plots, box plots, and scatter plots.

NM-DATA.6-8.3

Develop and evaluate inferences and predictions that are based on data.

1. Use observations about differences between two or more samples to make conjectures about the populations from which the samples were taken.
2. Make conjectures about possible relationships between two characteristics of a sample on the basis of scatter plots of the data and approximate lines of fit.
3. Use conjectures to formulate new questions and plan new studies to answer them.

NM-DATA.6-8.4

Understand and apply basic concepts of probability.

1. Understand and use appropriate terminology to describe complementary and mutually exclusive events.
2. Use proportionality and a basic understanding of probability to make and test conjectures about the results of experiments and simulations.
3. Compute probabilities for simple compound events, using such methods as organized lists, tree diagrams, and area models.

Problem Solving

NM-PROB.PK-12.1

Build new mathematical knowledge through problem solving.

NM-PROB.PK-12.2

Solve problems that arise in mathematics and in other contexts.

NM-PROB.PK-12.3

Apply and adapt a variety of appropriate strategies to solve problems.

NM-PROB.PK-12.4

Monitor and reflect on the process of mathematical problem solving.

Reasoning & Proof

NM-PROB.REA.PK-12.1

Recognize reasoning and proof as fundamental aspects of mathematics.

NM-PROB.REA.PK-12.2

Make and investigate mathematical conjectures.

NM-PROB.REA.PK-12.3

Develop and evaluate mathematical arguments and proofs.

NM-PROB.REA.PK-12.4

Select and use various types of reasoning and methods of proof.

Communication

NM-PROB.COMM.PK-12.1

Organize and consolidate their mathematical thinking through communication.

NM-PROB.COMM.PK-12.2

Communicate their mathematical thinking coherently and clearly to peers, teachers, and others.

NM-PROB.COMM.PK-12.3

Analyze and evaluate the mathematical thinking and strategies of others.

NM-PROB.COMM.PK-12.4

Use the language of mathematics to express mathematical ideas precisely.

Connections

NM-PROB.CONN.PK-12.1

Recognize and use connections among mathematical ideas.

NM-PROB.CONN.PK-12.2

Understand how mathematical ideas interconnect and build on one another to produce a coherent whole.

NM-PROB.CONN.PK-12.3

Recognize and apply mathematics in context and outside of mathematics.

Representation

NM-PROB.REP.PK-12.1

Create and use representations to organize, record, and communicate mathematical ideas.

NM-PROB.REP.PK-12.2

Select, apply, and translate among mathematical representations to solve problems.

NM-PROB.REP.PK-12.3

Use representations to model and interpret physical, social, and mathematical phenomena.

GRADES NINE–TWELVE

Number and Operations

NM-NUM.9-12.1

Understand numbers, ways of representing numbers, relationships among numbers and number systems.

1. Develop a deeper understanding of very large and very small numbers and various representations of them.
2. Compare and contrast the properties of numbers and number systems including the rational and real numbers, and understand complex numbers as solutions to quadratic equations that do not have real solutions.
3. Understand vectors and matrices as systems that have some of the properties of the real number system.
4. Use number-theory arguments to justify relationships involving whole numbers.

NM-NUM.9-12.2

Understand meanings of operations and how they relate to one another.

1. Judge the effects of such operations as multiplication, division, and computing powers and roots on the magnitudes of quantities.
2. Develop an understanding of properties of, and representations for, the addition and multiplication of vectors and matrices.
3. Develop an understanding of permutations and combinations and counting techniques.

NM-NUM.9-12.3

Compute fluently and make reasonable estimates.

1. Develop fluency in operations with real numbers, vectors, and matrices, using mental computation or paper and pencil calculations for simple cases and technology for more complicated cases.
2. Judge the reasonableness of numerical computations and their results.

Algebra

NM-ALG.9-12.1

Understand patterns, relations, and functions.

1. Generalize patterns using explicitly defined and recursively defined functions.
2. Understand relations and functions, and select and convert flexibly among and use various representations for them.
3. Analyze functions of one variable by investigating rates of change, intercepts, zeros, asymptotes, and local and global behavior.
4. Understand and perform transformations such as arithmetically combining, composing, and inverting commonly used functions, using technology to perform such operations on more complicated symbolic expressions.
5. Understand and compare the properties of classes of functions, including exponential, polynomial, rational, logarithmic, and periodic functions.
6. Intercept representations of functions of two variables.

NM-ALG.9-12.2

Represent and analyze mathematical situations and structures using algebraic symbols.

1. Understand the meaning of equivalent forms of expressions, equations, inequalities, and relations.
2. Write equivalent forms of equations, inequalities, and systems of equations and solve them with fluency—mentally or with paper and pencil in simple cases and using technology in all cases.
3. Use symbolic algebra to represent and explain mathematical relationships.
4. Use a variety of symbolic representations, including recursive and parametric equations, for functions and relations.
5. Judge the meaning, utility, and reasonableness of the results of symbol manipulations, including those carried out by technology.

NM-ALG.9-12.3

Use mathematical models to represent and understand quantitative relationships.

1. Identify essential quantitative relationship in a situation and determine the class or classes of functions that might model the relationships.

2. Use symbolic expressions including iterative and recursive forms, to represent relationship arising from various contexts.
3. Draw reasonable conclusions about a situation being modeled.

NM-ALG.9-12.4

Analyze change in various contexts.

1. Approximate and interpret rates of change from graphical and numerical data.

Geometry

NM-GEO.9-12.1

Analyze characteristics and properties of two- and three-dimensional geometric shapes and develop mathematical arguments about geometric relationships.

1. Analyze properties and determine attributes of two- and three-dimensional objects.
2. Explore relationships (including congruence and similarity) among classes of two- and three-dimensional geometric objects, make and test conjectures about them, and solve problems involving them.
3. Establish the validity of geometric conjectures using deduction, prove theorems, and critique arguments made by others.
4. Use trigonometric relationship to determine lengths and angle measures.

NM-GEO.9-12.2

Specify locations and describe spatial relationships using coordinate geometry and other representational systems.

1. Use Cartesian coordinates and other coordinate systems, such as navigational, polar, or spherical systems to analyze geometric situations.
2. Investigate conjecture and solve problems involving two- and three-dimensional objects represented with Cartesian coordinates.

NM-GEO.9-12.3

Apply transformations and use symmetry to analyze mathematical situations.

1. Understand and represent translations, reflections, rotations, and dilations of objects in the plane by using sketches, coordinates, vectors, function notations, and matrices.
2. Use various representations to help understand the effects of simple transformations and their compositions.

NM-GEO.9-12.4

Use visualization, spatial reasoning, and geometric modeling to solve problems.

1. Draw and construct representations of two and three-dimensional geometric objects using a variety of tools.
2. Visualize three-dimensional objects and spaces from different perspectives and analyze their cross sections.
3. Use vertex-edge graphs to model and solve problems.
4. Use geometric models to gain insights into and answer questions in other areas of mathematics.
5. Use geometric ideas to solve problems in and gain insights into other disciplines and other areas of interest such as art and architecture.

Measurement

NM-MEA.9-12.1

Understand measurable attributes of objects and the units, systems, and processes of measurement.

1. Make decisions about units and scales that are appropriate for problem situations involving measurement.

NM-MEA.9-12.2

Apply appropriate techniques, tools, and formulas to determine measurements.

1. Analyze precision, accuracy, and approximate error in measurement situations.
2. Understand and use formulas for the area, surface area, and volume of geometric figures, including cones, spheres, and cylinders.
3. Apply informal concepts of successive approximation, upper and lower bounds, and limit in measurement situations.
4. Use unit analysis to check measurement computations.

Data Analysis & Probability

NM-DATA.9-12.1

Formulate questions that can be addressed with data; collect, organize, and display relevant data to answer.

1. Understand the differences among various kinds of studies and which types of inferences can legitimately be drawn from each.
2. Know the characteristics of well-designed studies, including the role of randomization in survey and experiments.
3. Understand the meaning of measurement data and categorical data, of univariate and bivariate data, and of the term variable.
4. Understand histograms, parallel box plots, and scatter plots and use them to display data.
5. Compute basic statistics and understand the distinction between a statistic and parameter.

NM-DATA.9-12.2

Select and use appropriate statistical methods to analyze data.

1. For univariate measurement data, be able to display the distribution, describe its shape, and select and calculate summary statistics.
2. For bivariate measurement data, be able to display a scatter plot, describe its shape, and determine regression coefficients, regression equations, and correlation coefficients using technological tools.
3. Display and discuss bivariate data where at least one variable is categorical.
4. Recognize how linear transformations of univariate data affect shape, center, and spread.

5. Identify trends in bivariate data and find functions that model the data and transform the data so that they can be modeled.

NM-DATA.9-12.3

Develop and evaluate inferences and predictions that are based on data.

1. Use simulations to explore the variability of sample statistics from a known population and to construct sampling distributions.
2. Understand how sample statistics reflect the values of population parameters and use sampling distribution as the basis for informal inferences.
3. Evaluate published reports that are based on data by examining the design of the study, the appropriateness of the data analysis, and the validity of conclusions.
4. Understand how basic statistical techniques are used to monitor process characteristics in the workplace.

NM-DATA.9-12.4

Understand and apply basic concepts of probability.

1. Understand the concepts of sample space and probability distribution and construct sample spaces and distributions in simple cases.
2. Use simulations to construct empirical probability distributions.
3. Compute and interpret the expected value of random variables in simple cases.
4. Understand the concepts of conditional probability and independent events.
5. Understand how to compute the probability of a compound event.

Problem Solving

NM-PROB.PK-12.1

Build new mathematical knowledge through problem solving.

NM-PROB.PK-12.2

Solve problems that arise in mathematics and in other contexts.

NM-PROB.PK-12.3

Apply and adapt a variety of appropriate strategies to solve problems.

NM-PROB.PK-12.4

Monitor and reflect on the process of mathematical problem solving.

Reasoning & Proof

NM-PROB.REA.PK-12.1

Recognize reasoning and proof as fundamental aspects of mathematics.

NM-PROB.REA.PK-12.2

Make and investigate mathematical conjectures.

NM-PROB.REA.PK-12.3

Develop and evaluate mathematical arguments and proofs.

NM-PROB.REA.PK-12.4

Select and use various types of reasoning and methods of proof.

Communication

NM-PROB.COMM.PK-12.1

Organize and consolidate their mathematical thinking through communication.

NM-PROB.COMM.PK-12.2

Communicate their mathematical thinking coherently and clearly to peers, teachers, and others.

NM-PROB.COMM.PK-12.3

Analyze and evaluate the mathematical thinking and strategies of others.

NM-PROB.COMM.PK-12.4

Use the language of mathematics to express mathematical ideas precisely.

Connections

NM-PROB.CONN.PK-12.1

Recognize and use connections among mathematical ideas.

NM-PROB.CONN.PK-12.2

Understand how mathematical ideas interconnect and build on one another to produce a coherent whole.

NM-PROB.CONN.PK-12.3

Recognize and apply mathematics in context and outside of mathematics.

Representation

NM-PROB.REP.PK-12.1

Create and use representations to organize, record, and communicate mathematical ideas.

NM-PROB.REP.PK-12.2

Select, apply, and translate among mathematical representations to solve problems.

NM-PROB.REP.PK-12.3

Use representations to model and interpret physical, social, and mathematical phenomena.

Appendix B

Standards for the English Language Arts

by the International Reading Association and the National Council of Teachers of English

NLA.1

Students read a wide range of print and non-print texts to build an understanding of texts, of themselves, and of the cultures of the United States and the world; to acquire new information; to respond to the needs and demands of society and the workplace; and for personal fulfillment. Among these texts are fiction and nonfiction, classic and contemporary works.

NLA.2

Students read a wide range of literature from many periods in many genres to build an understanding of the many dimensions (e.g., philosophical, ethical, aesthetic) of human experience.

NLA.3

Students apply a wide range of strategies to comprehend, interpret, evaluate, and appreciate texts. They draw on their prior experience, their interactions with other readers and writers, their knowledge of word meaning and of the other texts, their word identification strategies, and their understanding of textual features (e.g., sound-letter correspondence, sentence structure, context, graphics).

NLA.4

Students adjust their use of spoken, written, and visual language (e.g., conventions, style, vocabulary) to communicate effectively with a variety of audiences and for different purposes.

NLA.5

Students employ a wide range of strategies as they write and use different writing process elements appropriately to communicate with different audiences for a variety of purposes.

NLA.6

Students apply knowledge of language structure, language conventions (e.g., spelling and punctuation), media techniques, figurative language, and genre to create, critique, and discuss print and non-print texts.

NLA.7

Students conduct research on issues and interests by generating ideas and questions, and by posing problems. Gather, evaluate, and synthesize data from a variety of sources (e.g., print and non-print texts, artifacts, people) to communicate discoveries in ways that suit purpose and audience.

NLA.8

Students use a variety of technological and information resources (e.g., libraries, databases, computer networks, video) to gather and synthesize information and to create and communicate knowledge.

NLA.9

Students develop an understanding of and respect for diversity in language use, patterns, and dialects across cultures, ethnic groups, geographic regions, and social roles.

NLA.10

Students whose first language is not English make use of their first language to develop competency in the English language arts and to develop understanding of content across the curriculum.

NLA.11

Students participate as knowledgeable, reflective, creative, and critical members of a variety of literacy communities.

NLA.12

Students use spoken, written, and visual language to accomplish their own purposes (e.g., for learning, enjoyment, persuasion, and the exchange of information).

Appendix C

ASCA National Standards for School Counseling Programs

(Campbell and Dahir, 1997)

ACADEMIC

Standard A

Acquire the attitudes, knowledge, and skills that contribute to effective learning across the life span.

A1. Improve academic self-concept.

1. Articulate competence and confidence as a learner.
2. Display positive interest in learning.
3. Take pride in work and achievement.
4. Accept mistakes as essential to the learning process.
5. Identify attitudes and behaviors that lead to successful learning.

A2. Acquire skills for improving learning.

1. Apply time management and task management skills.
2. Demonstrate how affect and persistence positively affect learning.
3. Use communication skills to know when and how to ask for help when needed.
4. Apply knowledge and learning styles to positively influence school performance.

A3. Achieve school success.

1. Take responsibility for actions.

2. Demonstrate the ability to work independently and cooperatively with students.
3. Develop a broad range of interests and abilities.
4. Demonstrate dependability, productivity, and initiative.
5. Share knowledge.

Standard B

Complete school with the academic preparation essential to choose from a wide range of substantial postsecondary options, including college.

B1. Improve learning.

1. Demonstrate the motivation to achieve individual potential.
2. Learn and apply critical thinking skills.
3. Apply the study skills necessary for academic success at each level.
4. Seek information and support from faculty, staff, family, and peers.
5. Organize and apply academic information from a variety of sources.
6. Use knowledge of learning styles to positively influence school performance.
7. Become a self-directed and independent learner.

B2. Plan to achieve goals.

1. Establish challenging academic goals in elementary, middle, and high school.
2. Use assessment results in educational planning.
3. Develop and implement annual plan of study to maximize academic ability and achievement.
4. Apply knowledge of aptitudes and interests to goal setting.
5. Use problem-solving and decision-making skills to assess progress toward educational goals.
6. Understand the relationship between classroom performance and success in school.
7. Identify postsecondary options consistent with interests, achievement, aptitude, and abilities.

Standard C

Understand the relationship of academics to the world of work and to life at home and in the community.

C1. Relate school to life experiences.

1. Demonstrate ability to balance school, studies, extracurricular and leisure activities, and family life.
2. Seek co-curricular and community experiences to enhance the school experience.
3. Understand the relationship between learning and work.
4. Demonstrate an understanding of the value of lifelong learning in achieving life goals.
5. Understand school success is preparation for transition from student to community member.
6. Understand how school and academic achievement enhance career and vocational opportunities.

PERSONAL/SOCIAL

Standard A

Acquire the knowledge, attitudes, and interpersonal skills to help in understanding and respecting self and others.

A1. Acquire self-knowledge.

1. Develop positive attitudes toward self as a unique and worthy person.
2. Identify values, attitudes, and beliefs.
3. Learn the goal-setting process.
4. Understand change is a part of growth.
5. Identify and express feelings.
6. Distinguish between appropriate and inappropriate behavior.
7. Recognize personal boundaries, rights, and privacy needs.
8. Understand the need for self-control and how to practice it.

9. Demonstrate cooperative behavior in groups.
10. Identify personal strengths and assets.
11. Identify and discuss changing personal and social roles.
12. Identify and recognize changing family roles.

A2. Acquire interpersonal skills.

1. Recognize that everyone has rights and responsibilities.
2. Respect alternative points of view.
3. Recognize, accept, respect, and appreciate individual differences.
4. Recognize personal boundaries, rights, and privacy needs.
5. Recognize and respect differences in various family configurations.
6. Use effective communication skills.
7. Know that communication involves speaking, listening, and nonverbal behavior.
8. Learn how to make and keep friends.

Standard B

Make decisions, set goals, and take necessary action to achieve goals.

B1. Self-knowledge application.

1. Use a decision-making and problem-solving model.
2. Understand consequences of decisions and choices.
3. Identify alternative solutions to a problem.
4. Develop effective coping skills for dealing with problems.
5. Demonstrate when, where, and how to seek help for solving problems and making decisions.
6. Know how to apply conflict resolution skills.
7. Demonstrate a respect and appreciation for individual and cultural differences.
8. Know when peer pressure is influencing a decision.
9. Identify long- and short-term goals.
10. Identify alternative ways of achieving goals.
11. Use persistence and perseverance in acquiring knowledge and skills.
12. Develop an action plan to set and achieve realistic goals.

Standard C

Understand safety and survival skills.

C1. Acquire personal safety skills.

1. Demonstrate knowledge of personal information (e.g., telephone number, home address).
2. Learn about the relationship between rules, laws, safety, and protection of individual rights.
3. Learn about the differences between appropriate and inappropriate physical contact.
4. Demonstrate the ability to set boundaries, rights, and personal privacy.
5. Differentiate between situations requiring peer support and those requiring adult professional help.
6. Identify resource people in the school and community, and know how to seek their help.
7. Apply effective problem-solving and decision-making skills to make safe and healthy choices.
8. Learn about the emotional and physical dangers of substance use and abuse.
9. Learn how to cope with peer pressure.
10. Learn techniques for managing stress and conflict.
11. Learn coping skills for managing life events.

CAREER

Standard A

Acquire the skills to investigate the world of work in relation to knowledge of self and to make informed career decisions.

A1. Develop career awareness.

1. Develop skills to locate, evaluate, and interpret career information.
2. Learn about the variety of traditional and nontraditional occupations.
3. Develop an awareness of personal abilities, skills, interests, and motivation.

4. Learn how to interact and work cooperatively in teams.
5. Learn to make decisions.
6. Learn how to set goals.
7. Understand the importance of planning.
8. Pursue and develop competency in areas of interest.
9. Develop hobbies and vocational interests.
10. Balance between work and leisure.

A2. Develop employment readiness.

1. Acquire employability skills such as working on a team, problem-solving, and organizational skills.
2. Apply job readiness skills to seek employment opportunities.
3. Demonstrate knowledge about the changing workplace.
4. Learn about the rights and responsibilities of employers and employees.
5. Learn to respect individual uniqueness in the workplace.
6. Learn how to write a resume.
7. Develop a positive attitude toward work and learning.
8. Understand the importance of responsibility, dependability, punctuality, integrity, and effort at work.
9. Utilize time- and task-management skills.

Standard B

Employ strategies to achieve future career goals with success and satisfaction.

B1. Acquire career information.

1. Apply decision-making skills to career planning, course selection, and career transition.
2. Identify personal skills, interests, and abilities and relate them to current career choice.
3. Demonstrate knowledge of the career-planning process.
4. Know the various ways in which occupations can be classified.
5. Use research and information resources to obtain career information.
6. Learn to use the Internet to access career planning information.
7. Describe traditional and nontraditional career choices and how they relate to career choice.

8. Understand how economic and societal needs influence employment trends and future training.

B2. *Identify career goals.*

1. Demonstrate awareness of the education and training needed to achieve career goals.
2. Assess and modify their educational plan to support career.
3. Use employability–job readiness skills in internship, mentoring, shadowing, and other experiences.
4. Select course work that is related to career interests.
5. Maintain a career planning portfolio.

Standard C

Understand the relationship between personal qualities, education, training, and the world of work.

C1. *Acquire knowledge to achieve career goals.*

1. Understand the relationship between educational achievement and career success.
2. Explain how work can help to achieve personal success and satisfaction.
3. Identify personal preferences and interests influencing career choice and success.
4. Understand that the changing workplace requires lifelong learning and acquiring new skills.
5. Describe the effect of work on lifestyle.
6. Understand the importance of equity and access in career choice.
7. Understand that work is an important and satisfying means of personal expression.

C2. *Apply skills to achieve career goals.*

1. Demonstrate how interests, abilities, and achievements relate to achieving life goals.
2. Learn how to use conflict management skills with peers and adults.
3. Learn to work cooperatively with others as a team member.
4. Apply academic and employment readiness skills in work-based learning situations.

References

Agnew, T., Vaught, C., Getz, H., and Fortune, J. (2000). Peer group clinical supervision program fosters confidence and professionalism. *Professional School Counseling, 4,* 6–12.

American Association of School Administrators. (2007). Web site, www.aasa.org.

American Counseling Association. (1987). *School counseling: A profession at risk.* Alexandria, VA: Author.

American Counseling Association (2005). *Code of ethics and standards of practice.* Alexandria, VA: Author.

American Evaluation Association. (1994). Guiding principles for evaluators. *New Directions for Program Evaluation, 66,* 19–26.

American School Counselor Association. (2004). *Ethical standards for school counselors.* Alexandria, VA: Author.

American School Counselor Association. (2005). *The ASCA national model: A framework for school counseling programs* (2nd ed.). Alexandria, VA: Author.

Arbuckle, D. S. (1961). The conflicting functions of the school counselor. *Counselor Education and Supervision, 1,* 54–59.

Association for Assessment in Counseling and Education. (1998). *Competencies in assessment and evaluation for school counselors.* website: http://aace .ncat.edu

Astramovich, R. L., Coker, J. K., and Hoskins, W. J. (2005). Training school counselors in program evaluation. *Professional School Counseling, 9,* 49–55.

Auger, R. W. (2004). Responding to terror: The impact of September 11 on K–12 schools and schools' responses. *Professional School Counseling, 7,* 222–31.

Beale, A. V. (1995). Selecting school counselors: The principal's perspective. *The School Counselor, 42,* 211–17.

Blackman, L., Hayes, R. L., Reeves, P. M., and Paisley, P. O. (2002). Building a bridge: Counselor educator–school counselor collaboration. *Counselor Education and Supervision, 41,* 243–56.

Bloom, B. S. (1953). Thought processes in lectures and discussions. *Journal of General Education, 7,* 160–69.

Brown, D., and Trusty, J. (2005). The ASCA national model, accountability, and establishing causal links between school counselors' activities and student outcomes: A reply to Sink. *Professional School Counseling, 9,* 13–16.

Bryan, J. (2005). Fostering educational resilience and achievement in urban schools through school-family-community partnerships. *Professional School Counseling, 8,* 219–28.

Burnham, J. J., and Jackson, C. M. (2000). School counselor roles: Discrepancies between actual practice and existing models. *Professional School Counseling, 4,* 41–49.

Campbell, C. A., and Dahir, C. A. (1997). *Sharing the vision: The national standards for school counseling programs.* Alexandria, VA: American School Counselor Association Press.

Center for School Counseling Outcome Research (2000). Web site, www.umass.edu/schoolcounseling.

Chata, C. C., and Loesch, L. C. (2007). Future school principals' views of the roles of professional school counselors. *Professional School Counseling, 11,* 35–42.

Cooper, B. S. (2002). *Promises and perils facing today's superintendents.* New York: Rowman and Littlefield.

Council for Accreditation of Counseling and Related Educational Programs. (2001). *CACREP accreditation standards and procedures manual* (4th ed.). Alexandria, VA: Author.

Crutchfield, L. B., and Borders, L. D. (1997). Impact of two clinical peer supervision models on practicing school counselors. *Journal of Counseling and Development, 75,* 219–30.

Deck, M. D., Cecil, J. H., and Cobia, D. C. (1990). School counselor research as perceived by American School Counselor Association leaders: Implications for the profession. *Elementary School Guidance and Counseling, 25,* 12–20.

Dilley, J., Foster, W., and Bowers, I. (1973). Effectiveness ratings of counselors without teaching experience. *Counselor Education and Supervision, 13,* 24–29.

Education Trust, The (1997, February). *The national guidance and counseling reform program.* Washington, DC: Author.

Eschenauer, R., and Hayes, C. (2005). The transformative individual school counseling model: An accountability model for urban school counselors. *Professional School Counseling, 8,* 244–49.

Gee, D. E. (2005). The cornerstone of our freedom. *School Administrator, 62,* 44.

Gladding, S. T. (2001). *The counseling dictionary.* Upper Saddle River, NJ: Merrill–Prentice Hall.

Goddard, R. D., Hoy, W. K., and Woolfolk, H. A. (2000). Collective teacher efficacy: Its meaning, measure, and impact on student achievement. *American Educational Research Journal*, 37, (in italics) 479–507.

Guerra, P. (1998, April). Reaction to DeWitt Wallace grant overwhelming: Readers sound off on February *Counseling Today* article. *Counseling Today*, 13–20.

Gysbers, N. C. (2004). Comprehensive guidance programs: The evolution and accountability. *Professional School Counseling, 8,* 1–14.

Hardesty, P. H., and Dillard, J. M. (1994). Analysis of activities of school counselors. *Psychological Reports, 74,* 447–50.

Herlihy, B., Gray, N., and McCollum, V. (2002). Legal and ethical issues in school counselor supervision. *Professional School Counseling, 6,* 55–61.

Hobbs, B. B., and Collison, B. B. (1995). School-community agency collaboration: Implications for school counselors. *School Counselor, 43,* 58–65.

Houser, R. (1998). *Counseling and educational research.* Thousand Oaks, CA: Sage.

Joint Committee on Testing Practices. (2004). *Code of fair testing practices in education.* Washington, DC: Author.

Kaffenberger, C. J., Murphy, S., Bemak, F. (2006). School counseling leadership team: A statewide collaborative model to transform school counseling. *Professional School Counseling, 9,* 288–95.

Lieberman, A. (2004). Confusion regarding school counselor functions: School leadership impacts role clarity. *Education*, 3, (in italics) 552–59.

Marzano, R. J. (2004). *Building background knowledge for academic achievement: Research on what works in schools.* Alexandria, VA: Association for Supervision and Curriculum Development.

Milsom, A., and Bryant, J. (2006). School counseling departmental Web sites: What message do we send? *Professional School Counseling, 10,* 210–17.

Moles, O. C. (1993). Collaboration between schools and disadvantaged parents: Obstacles and openings. In N. Chavkin (ed.) *Families and schools in a pluralistic society.* Albany: State University of New York Press.

Myrick, R. D. (2003). Accountability: Counselors count. *Professional School Counseling, 6,* 174–89.

National Association of Elementary School Principals. (2007). Web site, http:www.naesp.org.

National Association of Secondary School Principals. (2006). Web site, http:www.nassp.org.

National Council of Teachers of English. (1996). Standards for the English language arts. Newark, DE: International Reading Association.

National Council of Teachers of Mathematics (2000). Principles and standards for school mathematics. Reston, VA: Author.

National Education Association (2006). Web site, www.nea.org.

No Child Left Behind Act of 2001, Pub. L. No. 107–110.

Olson, M. J., and Allen, D. N. (1993). Principals' perceptions of the effectiveness of school counselors with and without teaching experience. *Counselor Education and Supervision, 33,* 10–21.

Page, B. J., Pietrzak, D. R., and Sutton, J. M. (2001). National survey of school counselor supervision. *Counselor Education and Supervision, 41,* 142–51.

Paisley, P. O., and Hayes, R. L. (2002). Transformations in school counselor preparation and practice. *Counseling and Human Development, 35,* 1–10.

Paisley, P. O., and Hayes, R. L. (2003). School counseling in the academic domain: Transformations in preparation and practice. *Professional School Counseling, 6,* 198–205.

Peterson, J. S., Goodman, R., Keller, T., and McCauley, A. (2004). Teachers and non-teachers as school counselors: Reflections on the internship experience. *Professional School Counseling, 7,* 246–56.

Posavac, E. J., and Carey, R. G. (2003). *Program evaluation: Methods and case studies* (6th ed.). Upper Saddle River, NJ: Prentice Hall.

Poynton, T. A., and Carey, J. C. (2006). An integrative model of data-based decision making for school counseling. *Professional School Counseling, 10,* 121–31.

Schellenberg, R. (2007). Standards blending: Aligning school counseling programs with school academic achievement missions. *Virginia Counselors Journal, 29,* 13–20.

Schellenberg, R., Parks-Savage, A., and Rehfuss, M. (2007). Reducing levels of elementary school violence with peer mediation. *Professional School Counseling, 10,* 475–81.

Shoffner, M. F., and Williamson, R. D. (2000). Engaging preservice school counselors and principals in dialogue and collaboration. *Counselor Education and Supervision, 40,* 128–41.

Simpson, R. L., LaCava, P. G., and Graner, P. S. (2004). The No Child Left Behind Act: Challenges and implications for educators. *Intervention in School and Clinic, 40,* 67–76.

Sink, C. (2005). *Contemporary school counseling: Theory, research, and practice.* Boston: Houghton Mifflin.

Sutton, C. M. (2006). The leader's role in reaching universal success for all. *School Administrator, 63,* 47.

United States Department of Education. (1996). *Companion document: Crosscutting guidance for the Elementary and Secondary Education Act.* Washington, DC: Author.

United States Department of Education. (2004). *Helping practitioners meet the goals of No Child Left Behind.* Washington, DC: Author.

United States House of Representatives 109th Congress. (2005). House Report 109–143, Departments of Labor, Health and Human Services, and Education, and Related Agencies Appropriation Bill, 2006. Washington, DC: Library of Congress.

Van Horn, S. M., and Myrick, R. D. (2001). Computer technology and the 21st century school counselor. *Professional School Counseling, 5*, 124–30.

Vansteenkiste, M., Lens, W., and Deci, E. L. (2006). Intrinsic versus extrinsic goal contents in self-determination theory: Another look at the quality of academic motivation. *Educational Psychologist, 41*, 19–29.

Virginia Department of Education (2001). *Standards of learning*. Richmond, VA: Author.

Whiston, S. C., and Sexton, T. L. (1998). A review of school counseling outcome research: Implications for practice. *Journal of Counseling and Development, 76*, 412–26.

Zalaquett, C. P. (2005). Principals' perceptions of elementary school counselors' role and functions. *Professional School Counseling*, 8, (in italics), 451–58.

Index

AACE. *See* Association for Assessment in Counseling and Education

AASA. *See* American Association of School Administrators

ACA. *See* American Counseling Association

academic achievement, 1, 7, 9–11, 18; importance of program evaluation in demonstrating, 44, 49–50; role of school counselor in, 1–4, 9–11, 13, 16, 24–25, 27, 29–39, 73, 78–79, 81–82. *See also* educational specialist

academic-focused: paradigm, 3, 12–14, 23–26, 29, 67; pedagogy, 69–73; programming, 21–22, 31–39, 56, 67, 72, 73–78. *See also* standards blending

accountability, 1, 4–5, 10–11, 13, 21, 33, 49; data collection and reporting, 16, 41–43, 49–50, 56, 57, 67, 74, 86. *See also* School Counseling Operational Plan for Effectiveness (SCOPE), School Counseling Operational Report of Effectiveness (SCORE)

ACES. *See* Association for Counselor Education and Supervision

achievement gap, 1, 4–5, 11, 14, 25, 32, 49, 84; action plan for targeting (*see* action plan). *See also* standards blending

action plan, 4, 50, 55–60, 74–75, 82; for closing the achievement gap, 55–56. *See also* School Counseling Operational Plan for Effectiveness (SCOPE)

advisory council, 15

AEA. *See* American Evaluation Association

American Association of School Administrators (AASA), 5, 34; Center for System Leadership, 15; *Stand Up for Public Education*, 18

American Counseling Association (ACA), 2–3, 21; *Code of Ethics and Standards of Practice*, 47; *School Counseling: A Profession at Risk*, 2

American Evaluation Association (AEA), 47; "Guiding Principles for Evaluators," 47

45–46. *See also Counseling and Educational Research*
program evaluation, methods of: distal, 44–47; outcome, 42–44, 46–47; process, 43–44, 46, 48; proximal, 44–47, 61
Program Evaluation: Methods and Case Studies, 47
PTSRC. *See* Parent-Teacher-Student Resource Center

referral, 25–26, 42, 70
reform-minded leadership, 5–6, 14, 67. *See also* new vision
research-supported services, 1, 4–5, 20–22
resource center. *See* Parent-Teacher-Student Resource Center (PTSRC)
results reports, 4, 33, 50, 55–56, 60–66, 74–75, 82. S*ee also* School Counseling Operational Report of Effectiveness (SCORE)

SCDRS. *See* School Counseling Data Reporting System
school administrator and school counselor leadership alliance, 2, 12–13
School Counseling Data Reporting System (SCDRS), 53. *See also* School Counseling Operational Plan for Effectiveness (SCOPE); School Counseling Operational Report of Effectiveness (SCORE)
School Counseling Leadership Team (SCLT), 5–6
School Counseling Operational Plan for Effectiveness (SCOPE), 50, 51–60, 72, 75, 82; abbreviated instructions, 54–55; examples of,

51, 58–60; instructions for the use of, 52–60
School Counseling Operational Report of Effectiveness (SCORE), 50, 52–56, 60–66, 72, 75, 82; abbreviated instructions, 54–55; examples of, *53, 63–65*; instructions for the use of, 52, 54–63
school-counseling standards. *See American School Counselor Association*
school counselor: consumers of research, 20, 22, 42; dual roles of, 23–24, 39, 50, 81, 83–84, 86; producers of research, 42; roles and functions of, 3–4. *See also* educational specialist; mental health specialist
school improvement, 5, 11, 17, 20, 43, 72, 78, 82
SCLT. *See* School Counseling Leadership Team
SCOPE. *See* School Counseling Operational Plan for Effectiveness
SCORE. *See* School Counseling Operational Report of Effectiveness
small group counseling, 2, 19, 31, 34–38, 42, 75
stakeholders, 59, 66, 85, 87; collective ownership and support, 10, 15, 18–19, 22, 49–50, 56, 65–66; in establishing SCLT, 6; information dissemination, 71, 73, 75–78; meeting the needs of, 15–22, 28–29, 37, 41–42
standards-based curriculum, 1, 4, 13–14, 20, 31, 33, 36, 49–50. *See also* standards blending

standards blending: comprehensive
nature of, 27, 32–34, 38; in
counselor education, 70, 72;
direct and overt process of, 22,
32–33, 74–75; effectiveness of,
33; methods of delivery, 34. *See
also* classroom guidance lessons;
individual counseling; small
group counseling
standards blending, alignment
approach for: closing the
achievement gap, 32, 36–38, 70,
73; total student development, 24,
27, 38, 50, 56, 73, 75, 77;
universal academic achievement,
27, 31–39, 78
supervision. *See* counselor
supervision
systems-focused, 25, 67, 83–85;
paradigm, 3–7, 32, 49; pedagogy,
4, 67, 72–73; programming,
10–11, 15, 69. *See also*
comprehensive school counseling;
standards blending

systems integration, 13; AASA
Center for System Leadership, 15

teaching background/experience:
instructional competency, 30–31,
71; school counselor need for,
29–31
technology, 4, 7, 17, 29, 50, 72, 77;
electronic distribution, 66;
websites, 28–29, 75–76, 85
total student development. *See*
standards blending
Transforming School Counseling
Initiative (TSCI), 16, 23, 32;
new vision, 3–4, 11, 49, 71–72,
85
triangulation. *See* program evaluation
TSCI. *See* Transforming School
Counseling Initiative

universal academic achievement:
counselor education, 72; data
collection and reporting, 16, 82.
See also standards blending

About the Author

Dr. Rita Schellenberg is nationally recognized for her outstanding achievements in education and school counseling. Dr. Schellenberg received her training to become a school counselor at the College of William and Mary in Virginia. In addition to a Ph.D. in counselor education and supervision, and state licensure with endorsements in pre-K–12 school counseling, Dr. Schellenberg holds the credentials of National Certified Counselor (NCC) and National Certified School Counselor (NCSC). Dr. Schellenberg is published in both national and state peer-reviewed journals and presents at regional, state, and local counseling conferences on issues related to contemporary school counseling practices. In addition to serving as a professional school counselor at the elementary and secondary levels and a counselor educator at the doctoral level, Dr. Schellenberg engages in career counseling, educational research, and consulting.

DATE DUE
